THE
SHIPSTON-ON-STOUR BRANCH

THE
SHIPSTON–ON–STOUR
BRANCH

S.C. JENKINS and R.S. CARPENTER

ISBN 1 874103 34 8

Designed by Paul Karau
Printed by Amadeus Press, Huddersfield

Published by
WILD SWAN PUBLICATIONS LTD.
1-3 Hagbourne Road, Didcot, Oxon, OX11 8DP

CONTENTS

ACKNOWLEDGEMENTS

We must give special thanks to Dick Burge who kindly gave us access to his own research notes on the line. We would also like to express our gratitude to the following who have been of assistance in the preparation of this book: John Norris; John Smith of Lens of Sutton; Chris Turner; staff of the Birmingham Reference Library; the Shakespeare Birthplace Trust, Stratford-on-Avon; University of Leicester Library; Warwick County Record Office; and the Westgate Library, Oxford.

Title page photo: A 1930s view of Stretton-on-Fosse.
L&GRP

This page: Stretton-on-Fosse station, looking south towards Moreton in the 1930s. *Lens of Sutton*

SHIPSTON-ON-STOUR 18. STATION ROAD AND STATION

Station Road soon after the turn of the century, with Shipston station in the background. In the 1930s, when the railway lorry from Moreton called at the station to deliver and collect parcels, it was backed up this slope and then up the platform ramp for loading at the station building. When Harold Hall served at Shipston station as a porter during the 1930s, he lodged in the third cottage from the left with Mr. and Mrs. Peachey and their four boys. The boys slept in one room in two double beds whilst Harold had "the small room at the back". "I had all my meals cooked and the washing done for twelve shillings a week. Mrs. Peachey's baked rabbit was the best I have ever tasted". Her husband worked at Mayo's wood yard. Mrs. Peachey's mother and brother, Tom Saunders, lived next door in the last house. Tom worked for Hutchings, the coal merchant. Harold Hall says the first cottage on the left was occupied by a retired station master but he could not recall his name.

Packer, cty. Alan Brain

INTRODUCTION

THE 9 mile long, single-track branch from Moreton-in-Marsh to Shipston-on-Stour is perhaps one of the Great Western's most neglected rural lines. Its history is nevertheless long, if somewhat obscure. Indeed, the branch originated back in the 1820s, when the pioneer railway promoter William James of Henley-in-Arden formulated an ambitious scheme for a system of horse tramways linking the Midlands canal system at Stratford to the Thames at Eynsham. If fully implemented this project would have enabled goods to be taken to Stratford by narrow boat and then sent down by rail to Eynsham Wharf, from where barges could carry coal and industrial products to London via the river. Powers were obtained in 1821, and a 16 mile 'main line' from Stratford to Moreton-in-Marsh was opened on 5th September 1826. A 2 mile branch from Ilmington to the small town of Shipston-on-Stour was opened in 1836.

The Stratford & Moreton tramway was essentially a product of the canal age, and the development of steam railways in the 1830s rapidly made it obsolete. William James himself knew this, for although the tramway had been his own brainchild, he did not hesitate to support the new railways - he was in fact one of the promoters of the Liverpool & Manchester Railway.

There were, by the 1830s, already plans for a steam-worked railway from Worcester to Oxford, and these plans eventually found tangible form as the Oxford, Worcester & Wolverhampton Railway. The OW & WR opened its main line from Evesham to Oxford in May 1853, and in the next few years the horse tramway functioned as a branch of the OW & WR.

In 1859 the OW & WR opened a branch from Honeybourne to Stratford-upon-Avon, but the Stratford & Moreton line remained in use, forming a valuable transport link for the inhabitants of Shipston-on-Stour. The northern section between Longdon Road and Stratford eventually fell into disuse, but in 1889 the southern portion between Moreton and Shipston-on-Stour was upgraded and reopened as a conventional steam-worked branch line. Sadly, passenger services lasted only until 1929, though the Shipston branch survived for many years thereafter as a goods-only line.

Unfortunately, the story of this Warwickshire branch line is unusually difficult to elucidate, and much of its history remains shrouded in mystery. Many small, rural branches started life as independent companies, and the records of their board meetings provide ample material for local historians to work upon; the Shipston branch, in contrast, was opened by a large main line company and there is no readily-available body of historical data – only odd snippets scattered at random throughout the voluminous Great Western archives. Furthermore, the branch lost its passenger service at a relatively early date and, although there are still many people who remember the railway before 1929, memories have inevitably dimmed with the passage of time, and there is no reliable body of oral evidence with which to supplement the meagre official sources. On the other hand, the long pre-history of this unusual line can be traced back to the Georgian era, and by incorporating material discovered in OW & WR archives it has been possible to compile a readable account of the line over a surprisingly long period. Paucity of documentary evidence has resulted in a few unresolved questions, but it is hoped that this short history will do much to fill a gap in the literature relating to Great Western branch lines.

In general, the narrative follows a chronological framework, enabling chapters 1, 2 and 3 to be devoted to the S & MR, OW & WR and early Great Western periods respectively, while chapter 4 continues the historical section of the story by covering the years of decline from 1914 until 1948. The next chapter describes the route of the line in detail, while the concluding chapter outlines the last, twilight years, from 1948 until closure in 1960.

A Note on County Boundaries

Historically, Shipston-on-Stour was situated at the meeting point of no less than four English counties, Warwickshire, Worcestershire, Gloucestershire and Oxfordshire. To prevent confusion it is perhaps worth mentioning that the parish of Shipston was a *detached* portion of Worcestershire, bounded on the west by the Warwickshire parishes of Whitchurch, Ilmington and Stretton-on-Fosse, and on the east by the Warwickshire parishes of Halford, Honington and Barcheston. The parish to the north of Shipston was part of Worcestershire, while areas of land to the south of the town were formerly parts of Oxfordshire and Gloucestershire; the Four Shires Stone near Moreton-in-Marsh was a famous meeting place of four counties. Today, Shipston-on-Stour is part of Warwickshire, and the Four Shires Stone now stands at the juncture of just three counties.

S. C. Jenkins
R. S. Carpenter

A tranquil scene in Shipston-on-Stour, looking towards the parish church of St. Edmund, which was rebuilt in 1854 by the architect G. E. Street. The stone-built houses on the right have now been demolished or rebuilt.

National Railway Museum

CHAPTER ONE

THE HORSE TRAMWAY
(1820 - 1847)

RIVERS were the highways of pre-industrial Britain, and in an age when decent roads did not exist, intrepid barge masters managed to prod, pole or haul their cumbersome vessels along many miles of barely-navigable waterway. In summer, or in times of drought, barges might lie aground for several weeks, while in winter the untamed rivers became raging torrents, defying all attempts to move upstream against the current. Coastal navigation was an alternative means of transport for heavy goods, and the immense coastline of the British Isles, winding for mile upon mile around bays, headlands and estuaries, provided ample numbers of convenient ports and harbours.

Canals were merely extensions of natural waterways, and, as the pace of industrialisation gathered momentum towards the end of the 18th century, large numbers of these new, man-made 'navigations' were constructed; some, such as the Leeds & Liverpool, were seen as coast-to-coast links, while others – particularly those in the English Midlands – were essentially links between existing waterways, opening up vital lines of internal communication. By 1800 there were about 3,000 miles of navigable waterway in England, approximately one third of which had been built between 1760 and the end of the century. Ambitious internal voyages became possible, and with coastal transport hampered by the impressment of merchant seamen for service in the Royal Navy, goods could be sent, for example, from London to Liverpool or from Bristol to Hull by *inland* waterways.

The Georgian canal system was relatively complex, but there were several gaps in the network, particularly where navigations were obstructed by intervening areas of high land. To solve this problem, Georgian canal engineers built connecting tramways such as the Surrey Iron Railway between the Thames at Wandsworth and the Croydon Canal. Opened in 1803, the Surrey Iron Railway had an especial significance in that it was an independent carrier, not owned by any canal or mining undertaking. It therefore looked to the future – towards a time when railways would replace waterways as the primary national transport system.

Although the first railway locomotive was built by Richard Trevithick in 1804, horses remained for many years the usual motive power on most contemporary tramways. There were nevertheless ambitious schemes for whole systems of such lines, and William Jessop, the Surrey iron engineer, suggested that his original line might be extended southwards to Portsmouth in order to provide a vital strategic link between London and the naval dockyards. In the event, Nelson's victory at Trafalgar destroyed Napoleon's navy, lifting the threat to Channel shipping and making the Portsmouth scheme unnecessary. However, eventual victory over the French engendered a period of national confidence in which engineers, industrialists and visionaries formulated a variety of grandiose canal and tramway schemes; one of these visionaries was William James of Henley-in-Arden.

A RAILWAY PIONEER

William James (1771-1837) is something of a shadowy figure. He can, however, be seen as one of the key figures in the evolution of railways, and some say that he should be considered along with George Stephenson, as a 'Father of the Railways'. Born on 13th June 1771, he obtained a good education, and started his working life as a solicitor, eventually becoming land agent for the Earl of Warwick. A wide range of personal and professional contacts (coupled with an intimate knowledge of the laws relating to land transactions) enabled him to indulge in various speculative activities, and in this capacity he became a successful colliery owner and canal promoter, with extensive mining interests in the South Staffordshire coalfield.

James would have been familiar with the short-distance tramroads used in many 18th century mining areas, and this personal knowledge may have kindled an enthusiasm for long-distance public railways which led him, in the early 1820s, to formulate plans for a 'Central Junction Railway or Tramroad'. This ambitious scheme envisaged a main line linking the Midlands canal system at Stratford-upon-Avon with the River Thames at Oxford, with a continuation extending south westwards to London. Additionally, branches would extend westwards to join the Gloucester & Cheltenham Railway, southwards to meet the Wilts & Berks Canal, and eastwards to join the Oxford and Coventry canals. The tramway main line would commence at the canal basin in Stratford, then follow the Stour Valley towards Moreton-in-Marsh. Beyond, the suggested route followed the Evenlode Valley via Shipton-under-Wychwood and Charlbury, a course later taken by the Oxford Worcester & Wolverhampton Railway.

In 1821, James surveyed a separate scheme for 'an engine railroad from Bishops Stortford to Clayhithe Sluice with a branch to Waddon' which, if built, could have provided useful transport facilities over a large part of Cambridgeshire.

These diverse schemes were, perhaps, over-ambitious for their time, and the Central Tramroad, if built in its entirety, would have been at a disadvantage in that it competed with two existing routes to London (the Oxford Canal and the Grand Junction Canal). A horse tramway was little faster than a competing canal, and was in fact at a *disadvantage* when handling bulk cargoes. On the other hand, the concept of a shorter line which would supplement (rather than duplicate) existing canals and work in conjunction with them was particularly attractive to people living in the relatively hilly areas south of Stratford-upon-Avon, and in August 1820

William James and other interested parties held a public meeting in Moreton-in-Marsh to discuss a proposed sixteen mile line between Stratford and Moreton.

FORMATION OF THE STRATFORD & MORETON RAILWAY COMPANY

A month later, in September 1820, a prospectus was issued in which it was suggested that coal might be carried on such a line for as little as five shillings per ton; the prospectus stated that the railway could be built at a cost of £40,000, and would yield 'ample interest' on that sum.

Supporters of the Stratford and Moreton scheme included (in addition to William James) prominent landowners such as Lord Redesdale of Batsford Park, colliery owners such as Lord Ward of Dudley, and local traders such as John Brewin and John Greaves.

John Freeman Mitford, the first Baron Redesdale (1748-1830), was undoubtedly the line's most important supporter; 'a sallow man, with round face and blunt features', he had obtained possession of the Batsford Estate (near Moreton-in-Marsh) in 1808, after serving as Lord Chancellor of Ireland. A noted reactionary who argued that liberality threatened the British Empire, Lord Redesdale was also an enthusiastic anti-Catholic who made no secret of his view that the abolition of the Catholic Church 'would alone bring peace to Ireland'. His Lordship was, on the other hand, prepared to support local causes such as the restoration of Batsford Church (which he rebuilt in 1822), and his willingness to encourage a novel venture such as the Stratford & Moreton Railway shows that the first Lord Redesdale was a more complex, and indeed more generous character than might be expected.

Well supported by Lord Redesdale, the Stratford & Moreton promoters prepared a Bill for submission to Parliament, and on 26th February 1821 *The Journal of the House of Commons* noted that, the standing orders 'relative to Bills for Making Railways' having been complied with, 'leave had been given to bring in a Bill for making and maintaining a railway or tramroad from Stratford-upon-Avon in the County of Warwick, to Moreton-in-Marsh in the County of Gloucester, with a branch to Shipston-on-Stour'.

The Bill was read for the first time on 5th March 1821 and then 'ordered to be read a second time'. There was, however, considerable opposition to the proposed railway, and several organisations or individuals petitioned against the scheme; on 11th April 1821, for example, petitions were received from 'the Mayor, Alderman, Burgesses and other inhabitants of the Borough of Evesham' and from 'the commissioners for the widening and repairing or rebuilding the bridge over the River Avon at or near Stratford-upon-Avon'. Other petitions were received from George Wigley Perrott and Mrs Jane Perrott, the 'widow of the late George Perrott', both of whom opposed the railway, and on 14th May 1821 *The Journal of the House of Commons* reported that:

'Two petitions, of William James, of Boswell Court, in the City of Westminster and of Warwick, land agent; and of several other inhabitants and occupiers of lands in Shipston-on-Stour, in the County of Worcester, and Moreton-in-Marsh, in the County of Gloucester, and in the neighbourhood of those places – were presented and read; taking notice of the Bill for making and maintaining a railway or tramroad from Stratford-upon-Avon, in County of Warwick, to Moreton-in-Marsh, in the County of Gloucester, with a branch to Shipston-on-Stour, in the County of Worcester, and praying that the same may not pass into law as it now stands'.

It is, at first glance, surprising that William James should have felt compelled to oppose the Bill at this stage in the proceedings, but in reality James seems to have objected to certain changes relating to the Shipston branch, and his petition was designed to amend the Bill rather than obstruct its passage through Parliament.

These petitions did not, in the event, present major problems, and on 16th May 1821 the Stratford & Moreton Railway Bill was sent up to the House of Lords. The Bill was examined by a Lords committee in the next few days, but this was merely a formality, and on 28th May the following message was delivered to the House of Commons by the Yeoman Usher of the Black Rod:

'Mr Speaker,
The Lords, authorised by virtue of His Majesty's Commissions for declaring his Royal Assent to several Acts agreed upon by both Houses, do desire the immediate attendance of this Honourable House to the House of Peers, to hear the Commission read.'

Accordingly the Speaker, together with those MPs still sitting in the House, went up to the House of Lords, and when they returned the Speaker reported that the Royal Assent had been given to 'several public and private Bills' - among them the Stratford & Moreton Railway Bill.

The newly-passed Act (1 & 2 George IV cap 63) incorporated William James, Lord Redesdale, Lord Ward of Dudley, and fifty-four others as the Stratford & Moreton Railway, and together, these gentlemen were empowered to begin construction of a sixteen mile line between Stratford-upon-Avon and Moreton-in-Marsh.

The authorised capital was £33,500, and the Act set a time limit of five years for completion of the works. Clauses were inserted for the protection of turnpike trusts, and it was stated that, where the tramway ran beside a turnpike road a space of at least 35ft was to be left for the passage of road traffic; no tolls would be paid by the tramway to the trustees of such turnpikes.

The Act enabled the Stratford & Moreton Railway proprietors to build their 'railway or tramroad from Stratford-upon-Avon, in the County of Warwick, to Moreton-in-Marsh, in the County of Gloucester, with a branch to Shipston-on-Stour, in the County of Worcester'. The authorised route commenced at the Stratford Canal basin, on the north bank of the River Avon, and crossed the river before heading due south along the Stour Valley. Running via Atherstone and Alderminster, it reached higher land near Ilmington and surmounted a summit of 350ft before descending abruptly to the valley of the Knee Brook. Beyond, the planned route climbed once again to reach an elevation of over 400ft at Moreton-in-Marsh.

Civil engineering would be comparatively heavy, with substantial cuttings, several embankments, a tunnel near Stretton-on-Fosse and a major river crossing at Stratford-upon-Avon. From Stratford to Newbold-on-Stour, a distance of 6 miles, the line would run beside the Stratford to Shipston turnpike (now the A34).

THE CHOICE OF RAIL, GAUGE AND MOTIVE POWER

When first planned, it is likely that the promoters had intended to build a 'plateway', with 'L'-shaped cast-iron rails resting on rectangular stone blocks. The Surrey Iron Railway, Peak Forest Tramway, Lancaster Canal Tramroad and other early lines all employed this form of trackwork, which was designed to accommodate vehicles with flangeless wheels, the flange being on the rails rather than on the wheels.

Before making a final decision on this important matter, James toured the country looking at various other railways, tramways and colliery lines, and during these travels he visited Bledlington Ironworks in Northumberland to see the wrought-iron rails which had recently been invented by John Birkenshaw, the works manager. Available in lengths up to 18ft, these fish-bellied rolled iron rails were far superior to any form of iron plateway, and many famous engineers, including George Stephenson, had seen the rails in use on the local tramway. James was immediately converted to the new system, and in June 1821 he proclaimed: 'Light has at length shone from the north, and I pronounce as my decided opinion that the malleable iron rail road at Bledlington Works is by far the best I have seen both in respect of its material and its form'.

Needless to say, when James returned to Warwickshire he was full of praise for Birkenshaw's fish-bellied iron rails and, at a meeting of shareholders held at Moreton-in-Marsh on 13th July 1821, he persuaded his fellow proprietors to use the new rails on their tramway. Explaining how, in his travels, he had examined many railways 'in Somersetshire, the Forest of Dean, South Wales, Staffordshire, Shropshire, Lancashire and Northumberland', he declared that he preferred 'the malleable to the cast iron as a material for the rail, on account of its superior strength, facility and cheapness of construction, security from accidents, and the necessity of repairs'. Anticipating the widespread introduction of continuous welded rail, he suggested that 'by welding pieces together the railway may be laid even for miles without a joint'.

Sagacious businessman that he was, James did not perhaps make it entirely clear that he had made an agreement with George Stephenson, under the terms of which he would give 'his best assistance for the using and employment of locomotive engines south of an imaginary line drawn from Liverpool to Hull'. In effect, William James had become a sort of sales representative for Stephenson's engines in Southern England, and his efforts to introduce the latest rails must be seen as an essential first step towards the introduction of steam locomotives.

Not surprisingly, James was keen to recommend the use of locomotives on the tramway, and having spoken at length on the advantages of Birkenshaw's rails he spoke in favour of George Stephenson's locomotives which, he claimed, were 'the most perfect' engines available. The relevant section of his report may be worth quoting in full:

'The employment of locomotive engines on the railway is a subject of vital importance as it respects the prospect of profit to the company and of benefit to the public. Of the powers of the company to permit the use of engines on the railway, I have no doubt whatever on the subject, indeed it might with great plausibility be contended that no other mode of draft was ever contemplated. On this subject I confess I kept a steady view during the progress of the Bill through Parliament and my sentiments upon the excellence of communications by rail road worked by steam engines have long been known to many gentlemen present.'

Another related, and equally important, result of William James's visit to the North East, and his meetings with Stephenson, may have been the choice of gauge. Hitherto there had been great diversity in the gauge of tramways and plateways. The Peak Forest Tramway (and other lines engineered by James Outram) had a gauge of 4ft 2½ins, while the Surrey Iron Railway was a 4ft 2in gauge line. The Penydarren Tramway, meanwhile, had adopted a gauge of 4ft 4ins. Significantly, William James selected Stephenson's preferred gauge of 4ft 8½ins, making the Stratford & Moreton Railway one of the very first lines to use this now familiar 'standard gauge'. It should not, however, be forgotten that the axle length of most English farm wagons was also around 4ft 8ins.

CONSTRUCTING THE TRAMWAY

Although James was himself an accomplished engineer, the line was actually built with the help and advice of two better known engineers – Thomas Telford (1757-1834) and John Urpeth Rastrick (1780-1856). Telford, who had already engineered the Holyhead Road, the Caledonian Canal, and countless lesser works, must have found the Stratford & Moreton Railway a relatively straightforward project, and in view of his vast experience and many other commitments, we must assume that he played a very small part during the construction of the line. His role was that of a consultant, and there is no evidence that he ever visited the works. Nevertheless, such was Telford's prestige that he was able to exert considerable influence in such important matters as the choice of motive power, and the fact that this respected engineer decided *against* the use of locomotives probably ensured that the tramway, when opened, was worked exclusively by horses.

J. U. Rastrick played a more active part in the construction of the tramway, and in his role of 'surveyor' to the company he was responsible for the design of bridges and many other engineering features. Rastrick (who in later years would achieve fame for his work as engineer to the Brighton Line) also advised against the use of locomotives, though he did not rule out their use at some later date. William James, meanwhile, was probably continuing to advise on technical matters relating to the design of trackwork and vehicles, though one feels that his restless temperament may have put him at a disadvantage when it came to solving practical engineering problems.

Tragically, James's premature vision of a nationwide system of tramways led to his financial downfall, and he was declared bankrupt in 1823. Thereafter his role in the affairs of the Stratford & Moreton Railway was considerably reduced, though he did not immediately retire from the scene.

Construction of the tramway was probably in full swing by 1823, and in the ensuing months the inhabitants of rural Warwickshire would no doubt have gazed in wonder at what to them appeared to be a stupendous feat of civil engineering. It is likely that the tramway was built by a predominantly local labour force, for although a sizeable canal system had already been constructed it had been built piecemeal over a relatively long period, and there was as yet no large, mobile force of skilled 'navvies' willing to move from place to place in search of work. Moreover, the work of construction progressed painfully slowly. In part, this may have been a result of labourers returning to agricultural work at harvest time, but William James's bankruptcy can have done little to inspire confidence in the project, and the company had difficulty in raising its authorised share capital.

The chosen route provided a good 'mix' of cuttings and embankments, enabling stone and infill to be obtained locally without recourse to expensive importation from other areas. Rails, chairs and rolling stock, however, were brought to Stratford via the Stratford Canal, the existence of which was clearly an immense advantage to Rastrick during the later stages of construction.

As we have seen, James had urged the use of Birkenshaw's rails, which were made at Bledlington, some 250 miles north of Stratford. Without water transport they would never have reached Warwickshire. On the other hand, it is possible that some of the rails were rolled elsewhere, perhaps at the works of Bradley, Foster, Rastrick & Co of Stourbridge. Rastrick was the managing partner in this firm, and may have decided to roll the rails himself, putting extra money in his own pocket, but at the same time reducing transport costs. Significantly there *is* a local tradition that some S & M trackwork was manufactured in Stourbridge. On a footnote, it is of interest to note that in 1828 Foster and Rastrick achieved lasting fame by building the *Stourbridge Lion*, the first locomotive to run in the United States of America.

As far as can be ascertained, the tramway's horse-drawn wagons were built in Liverpool by Smith & Willey, whose foundry was situated on the corner of Smithdown Road and Falkner Street. Surviving vehicles all contain ironwork from this manufacturer.

THE OPENING OF THE TRAMWAY

The tramway was more or less complete by the summer of 1826, the work of construction having taken around four years. Although by later standards of railway construction this

was a long time, it is worth noting that the Stratford & Moreton Railway had been built more rapidly than most canals – the neighbouring Oxford Canal, for example, had taken 21 years to complete, while the Leeds & Liverpool had taken no less than 46 years to finish.

In August 1826 notices were placed in *Jackson's Oxford Journal* and other local papers, informing the general public that 'the railroad from Stratford-on-Avon to Moreton-in-Marsh' would be opened 'for the carriage of coal, corn, timber and all other minerals' on Tuesday, 5th September. It was also announced that on the same day Moreton-in-Marsh market would be revived, the implication being that, with improved transport facilities, Moreton would be able to develop as an important regional centre.

Opening Day was treated as a public holiday in Moreton-in-Marsh, and people from the surrounding countryside converged upon the little town in large numbers, the gentry riding in carriages or on horseback while the ordinary folk tramped in on foot. The line had already become one of the local wonders, the tunnel under Campden Road and the impressive viaduct at Stratford being particular talking points. Happily, it is possible to reconstruct the events of that historic day with the aid of eyewitness accounts which appeared in *Jackson's Oxford Journal* and *The Warwick Advertiser* just four days later. The Journal told its readers that:

'An immense concourse of persons attended . . . the opening of the railroad leading . . . from Stratford-upon-Avon on Tuesday last. All were not led by curiosity; a respectable number attended for the purpose of business, and it was their unanimous opinion that Moreton, from its situation, and the facility of communication which it now possesses with the manufacturing districts, must become a considerable mart for corn . . . In the course of the morning the committee under whose superintendence the railroad has been completed, accompanied by bands of music, arrived in one of the road wagons, preceding several others laden with coal, coke, deal, planks, grindstones, and other articles of merchandise required in the neighbourhood. They afterwards dined together at the Unicorn Inn . . . The innkeepers had more mouths to feed than bread and meat to fill them with; but they were not in fault . . . thousands more attended than any reasonable person could have looked for. In saying that a fat ox was roasted entire, after the above it need hardly be added that its bones were picked clean.'

The Warwick Advertiser recorded that the tramway's main supporters rode in 'five covered carriages, preceded by a band of music and followed by twenty-one carriages laden with coals, timber, lime and merchandise'. This great convoy left Stratford at ten o'clock in the morning, and arrived, presumably, at some time in the early afternoon. The crowds waiting at Moreton were so big that the ceremonial procession could not immediately enter the terminus; 'competent judges', suggested the *Advertiser*, estimated that 'there were not less than 20,000 persons present'. After the ox roast, continued the paper:

'The committee sat down to an elegant dinner at the Unicorn Inn . . . the Right Hon. Lord Redesdale in the chair. His Lordship presided with great urbanity. The day was spent with the greatest conviviality, and the company, consisting of several gentlemen of the counties of Gloucester, Warwick and Stafford, mostly proprietors, did not separate till a late hour.

'Thus was celebrated an event, which it is to be hoped, will provide a blessing to the poor in that neighbourhood as affording the means of their being supplied with fuel, as well as the necessities of life, at a much cheaper rate than hitherto could be afforded. Indeed, the railroad promises to be of the greatest advantage to the whole of the country through which it passes, and particularly to Moreton and its neighbourhood. Some of the carriages returned the same day, laden with grain.

'The distance from Stratford to Moreton is 16 miles, making a journey of 32 miles, which was easily performed by the same horses. The ease and expedition with which passengers can be conveyed upon this railroad has induced some spirited individuals to propose establishing a daily coach . . . Universal admiration and surprise were excited and warmly expressed by the spectators on seeing three remarkably fine horses, the property of Messrs Greaves & Son, drawing a weight exceeding 15 tons in four large coal-loaded waggons along the line, even where there was the steepest ascent, without the least apparent extraordinary exertion; and this was the more to be admired as the carriages appeared quite new, the new axles consequently revolving less freely than those of the old ones.'

We are not, unfortunately, told if William James was allowed to ride in the first trains along with the rest of the committee. Bankruptcy was in 1826 a condition of total disgrace, and although James continued to survey tramways up and down the country – and was for a time referred to as 'Clerk to the Company' – he had at the time of the opening been replaced by J. Hanson. Reading between the lines, his presence must have been something of an embarrassment, and we can assume that by September 1826 he had been quietly removed from any position of prominence. If indeed he had witnessed the Grand Opening of the Stratford & Moreton Railway, the Great Day must, for him, have been a melancholy occasion.

INITIAL DIFFICULTIES
Although William James deserves to be remembered as a key figure in the origins of the Stratford & Moreton Railway, it is easy to overstate his role in the affairs of the company, and other personalities – notably Lord Redesdale, John Greaves and John Rastrick – cannot be ignored. It is nevertheless significant that James's untimely fall was mirrored by a downturn in the tramway's fortunes, and things were, in truth, not the same after his departure. This was mainly a result of the company's severe financial problems which, in turn, stemmed from continuing difficulties in raising share capital.

It was estimated that the proprietors had spent up to £80,000 on their 16 mile line, thereby incurring huge debts which could not be repaid out of revenue. Moreover, the tramway had been opened before its works were properly complete, presumably in the hope that tolls from coal and corn traffic would help to pay off some of the debts. In 1827 it was stated that much expense had been incurred simply to keep the line open, and there had been many problems 'where there were deep cuttings and high embankments'. However, receipts were on the whole favourable and takings from 5th September 1826 to 31st July 1827 totalled £2,256, including £66 from 'the weighing machine'; the next five months, from 31st July until 31st January, produced an income of £1,385.

Sadly, expenditure was consistently higher than income, and in February 1828 Benjamin Baylis, a Stratford coal merchant, produced a damning report on the state of the line:

'On inspecting the road, I find it in a very imperfect state; the greater part will want taking up and relaying, as the blocks were bedded upon the natural earth instead of a casing of gravel or broken stone which, through all the deep cuttings should have been six inches thick, and upon all the embankments four inches; this casing would have prevented the pressure of weight from displacing the rails, and also would have served as an underground drain (through all the deep cuttings) to have conveyed the water to the side drains, instead of which in many places the blocks have sunk nearly the whole depth in a soft clay.

'I find also the road between the blocks has been filled only in a temporary way, in consequence of which the track has become so weak, that in wet weather the horses travel in a trench of mud, which has no means of escaping and proves very injurious to the road.

'I find also that many of the blocks, chairs and sleepers are very imperfect. I propose to take out all the broken blocks . . . which at the present time amount to nearly two thousand blocks, upwards of six hundred wooden sleepers and a large number of iron chairs, and to place perfect ones in their places. The whole length of the road should be filled in with gravel or broken stone from four to six inches thick, which must be done before it will be firm and substantial.

'I find the slopes of the embankments and the cuttings are very much too upright, in many places they are not more than one foot horizontal to one foot perpendicular, which at least ought to have been twice as much. The embankment in Potters Valley has already slipped and I have reason to believe that nearly the whole of it will yet slip as its base is not in proportion to its height and evidently exhibits the appearance of being badly made.

'I find Ditchford embankment in a similar state, and several other places, and as it will be impossible for the embankment to be repaired and the slips got up without stoppage, great exertions should be made next summer (when the trade is not so great) to do them.

'I find the quick fences and post railing in a very bad state. In many places, quick has not been planted and in other places it has been so improperly done that I should propose taking it up, making fresh borders and replanting it. The posts and rails in many parts I find broken and decayed and must be replaced.'

It is, in retrospect, surprising that Baylis could find so *much* at fault just 17 months after the line had been opened, and it is possible that he was exaggerating any defects in an attempt to further his own ambitions; if so, Baylis was entirely successful, the immediate result of his report being the removal of Thomas Oakley, who had hitherto supervised the line on behalf of his employer John Rastrick. In his place the company appointed John Smith, an acquaintance of Baylis, to repair the sinking earthworks and inadequate track.

Once Smith had remedied these deficiencies, Benjamin Baylis was himself willing to lease the entire line, and on 1st November 1829 he took over the tramway at an initial rent of £2,100 pa. In return, Baylis undertook to maintain the line in good order and contribute £50 a year towards the salary of J. Hanson, the company clerk.

Under Baylis, the tramway at last began to show a profit, and in the first year of his rental, receipts amounted to £2,555 1s 5d, while expenses fell to £1,788 4s 3d. Thereafter the company's position improved progressively, and the proprietors were once again able to contemplate the possibility of extending their original line.

EXTENSION TO SHIPSTON

Extensions to Eynsham and Warwick had been surveyed prior to opening, and the 1825 Act had authorised a deviation of the planned branch to the town of Shipston-on-Stour. Unfortunately, the period of optimism following Napoleon's defeat had been followed by a period of unemployment, rising prices and trade depression, and in this uncertain economic climate the Shipston branch was not proceeded with.

Further powers were, however, sought in 1833, and with receipts from the original line running at a healthy £3,000 pa, the tramway's proprietors were determined that, on this occasion, the desired branch to Shipston-on-Stour would, at long last, be built.

In February 1833 the company deposited a Bill seeking 'a more convenient line of communication between the ... railway and Shipston-on-Stour', and this new Bill was read for the first time on 4th March 1833. After an easy passage through the Lower House, the Bill was sent up to the Lords, and finally, on 10th June 1833 the Act 'enabling the Stratford & Moreton Railway Company to make a new Branch of Railway to Shipston-on-Stour in the County of Worcester' received the Royal Assent.

The 1833 Act (3 William IV cap. 70) provided for the construction of a short branch from the original line 'at or near the nine and a quarter mile post from Stratford', to Brick-Kiln Close in Husbandman's End at Shipston-upon-Stour. Five years was allowed for completion of the works, and the Stratford & Moreton company was authorised to raise an additional £10,000 in order to finance the new branch.

On a footnote, it is interesting to note that the Act stipulated a gauge of not less than four feet between the inside edges of the rails, and this curious (though somewhat meaningless) provision seems to have given rise to the tradition that the Stratford & Moreton Railway was a four foot gauge line. There are, unfortunately, no other early references to the gauge of the Stratford & Moreton Railway and there must, in consequence, be an element of doubt on this important point; on the other hand, when the gauge was actually measured in 1851, it was found to be approximately 4ft 8½ins, and as there is no record of any regauging between 1826 and 1851 it is reasonable to conclude that the railway was laid to the Stephenson gauge throughout its lifetime.

In an improving business climate, the Shipston-on-Stour line was opened on 11th February 1836. Leaving the 'main line' at Ilmington Junction, this short branch ran due east to its destination and terminated on the northern side of Shipston. The new line could have formed the first part of any extension towards Warwick.

THE TRAMWAY IN OPERATION

The announcements made prior to opening in 1826 featured a scale of charges for various types of traffic, and is tabulated as follows:

TABLE 1: Rates of Tonnage on the S & M Railway
For coal, coke, culm, iron, lead & all other metals, hay & straw, flagstone and building materials ....2d per ton per mile
For corn, timber, deals, staves, lime, limestone, slates, peat, bricks & tiles ....1½d per ton per mile
For stone for building, pitching or paving stone in the rough, cinders, gravel or stone for making or repairing roads, ashes, sand, clay, manure, marl & chalk ....1d per ton per mile
For all other commodities, goods & merchandise not enumerated above ....4d per ton per mile

In common with contemporary turnpike trusts, the Stratford & Moreton Railway had a large number of nominal proprietors, but few of these gentlemen ever attended the company's 'General Assemblies' (which were often declared inquorate) and under these circumstances the tramway was managed by a handful of active proprietors, helped by the 'Surveyor' (ie engineer) and the 'Clerk to the Company'. Until the 1830s these positions were filled by J. U. Rastrick and J. Hanson respectively, but from 1834 until about 1869 most of the company's business was conducted by Hanson's successor, John Kershaw. In the absence of other officers the clerk was in effect the tramway manager and in this sense the term 'clerk' is something of a misnomer.

The tramway was operated by private carriers who provided both goods and (to a lesser extent) passenger services. From its inception, the line was worked on what might be called 'canal principles', with individual wagons in lieu of boats. With no signalling or telegraph to regulate the passage of these vehicles on the single line tramway, all movements took place during the hours of daylight; there were a large number of 'turn-outs' or short loops, allowing up and down wagons to pass en route. Cottages were dotted at intervals along the route of the tramway, and these acted as toll houses, at which payment was made for the right of passage; there were also one or two lineside inns which provided accommodation and refreshments for passing travellers. Carriers used their own horses and vehicles, some of which were licensed to carry passengers.

In its early days, the tramway was worked as an extension of the Stratford Canal, with services extending southwards from Stratford to Moreton and to Shipston-on-Stour. With no large industrial centres en route, and no connecting waterways at its southern terminals, traffic was sparse, though if the line had managed to reach either the Thames at Eynsham or some point on the canal system at Warwick or elsewhere it would clearly have attracted valuable through traffic.

Unfortunately, the original concept of a horse-worked tramway was becoming obsolete by the 1830s, and with steam railways being opened in increasing numbers it seemed unlikely that the tramway would ever be extended beyond its existing limits. By 1836, there were already plans for a steam railway linking Oxford and Worcester, while William James had himself become a promoter of the Liverpool & Manchester Railway.

With no through traffic, the tramway eked out a precarious existence carrying agricultural produce northwards to Stratford and modest amounts of coal southwards from Stratford Canal Basin to Moreton and Shipston. Red bricks from the Midlands and roofing slate from Wales may also have flowed southwards onto the route, and in this context it is noticeable that there are many brick buildings in Shipston, but very few in Moreton-in-Marsh.

SOME DETAILS OF THE TRAMWAY

The line was laid on rectangular stone blocks, spaced at approximately one yard intervals, and it is believed that the fish-bellied rails weighing 30lb per yard were delivered in 15ft sections, though there may have been some variation between different batches of rail. The chairs used to attach the rails to their blocks weighed 6lbs apiece and they were secured by two 5in spikes, resting in holes drilled into the stone. Oak 'rawlplugs' were inserted into the holes before the spikes were driven home. When first laid, iron cotter pins were employed to hold the rails in place, but this method – which may not have allowed for expansion in hot weather – was soon abandoned, and by the 1840s the rails were being wedged into place.

The original Bledlington rails were 'T'-shaped in section, and rested in their iron chairs with their broad flange uppermost. It is possible that, by 1844, the company was experimenting with the use of heavier-section rail which could be spiked directly to the stone sleepers with its flange acting as a secure base. By this method, chairs would not have been necessary. There were also some conventional wooden cross sleepers which may have been laid as an experiment, though in general on horse-worked lines it was preferable to use individual stone sleepers which did not inconvenience the horses. Moreover, wooden sleepers would have been splintered and damaged by the constant passage of iron-shod animals.

The tramway's wagons were small, 4-wheeled open vehicles, similar to those used on other early lines. They consisted of simple, box-like bodies resting on two stout sole bars which extended outwards at each end to form primitive buffers. The wooden bodies were fabricated from horizontal boards, strengthened by external wooden ribs. Surviving examples have projecting 'top raves' (which may have been fitted later) and a single hinged door at the rear. Unlike modern railway vehicles, their bodies were carried between the wheels, which were made of cast iron with hollow spokes. Prominent brake handles were fitted on one side, and these enabled the wagons to be braked by men walking alongside or drivers riding in the vehicles. Tramway regulations stipulated that each wagon had to display the name of its owner together with its individual number. In addition,

vehicles licenced to carry passengers carried a distinctive metal plate.

There were no stations as such on the Stratford & Moreton Railway, though passengers were probably picked up and set down at recognised stopping places such as inns, crossroads and villages. The intermediate passing loops may have been utilised for the loading and unloading of goods traffic, and there were wharves at Newbold-on-Stour, Ilmington and other intermediate places (which were presumably equipped with sidings).

Complex track layouts were provided only at the line's three terminals, and one of these, Stratford-upon-Avon, was inevitably the largest, with sidings diverging to serve coal wharves, timber stores and two canal basins. Stables and maintenance buildings were also provided, and there were similar though smaller facilities at both Moreton and Shipston. The tramway's buildings were built of Cotswold stone at Moreton, but elsewhere most structures utilised red brick.

THE DEATH OF WILLIAM JAMES

James continued to promote railways throughout the country but, having failed to recover his fortunes, he eventually moved, in semi-retirement, to Bodmin, where he eked out a living as an estate agent. Lord Redesdale, John Kirshaw and his other friends occasionally helped out by sending small cash gifts, and on 14th December 1836 he sent one last letter to Kirshaw, his former clerk. The letter was rambling and incoherent, suggesting that its unfortunate writer was already near to death:

> 'As to my general prospect, I think it has much improved within the last twelve months. I open an office in London on January 1st as a land agent and consulting engineer. I have three views into futurity which at present appear flattering, and as my unhappy children have disposed of every article of furniture and memorial of my name and family, I am, as it were, sold out by them, and I must begin the world anew. O God, I have been most cruelly treated, but no more.'

Three months later, on 10th March 1837, William Jones was dead. This Warwickshire pioneer had played an important role in the early history of Britain's railways, but true success was left to others, some of whom apparently made use of his pioneering work. James's surveys of the Liverpool & Manchester, for example, were later utilised by the Stephensons while his route for the Canterbury & Whitstable Railway was subsequently used by Joseph Locke who, as George Stephenson's assistant, had replaced James as engineer. Again, James's son took out a patent on the tubular boiler before the idea was used by the Stephensons, but they later managed to obtain all or most of the credit.

Today, William James is remembered chiefly as the engineer of the Stratford & Moreton Railway, but at the time of his death there is evidence that he *was* widely recognised as a 'Father of Railways', and in 1846 a subscription was raised for the benefit of his family. The Committee formed to raise this fund was led by George Rennie, Robert Stephenson, Joseph Locke and Isambard Kingdom Brunel, all of whom apparently appreciated James's pioneering work and mourned his passing.

Coincidentally, two other personalities who had been associated with the Stratford & Moreton Railway died in the 1830s. Thomas Telford, who died in 1834, had played a comparatively minor role in the company's affairs, but Lord Redesdale, who died in 1830, must rank with William James as a key figure in the S & MR story. His son, John Thomas Freeman-Mitford (1805-86), inherited the Batsford estate and

continued to take at least some interest in the railway. Indeed, the second Lord Redesdale took a particular interest in railways of all kinds as a result of his work as the chairman of numerous House of Lords committees, and this eccentric bachelor (who always 'wore an old fashioned tail coat') was destined to play an important, albeit reluctant, role in the affairs of the Oxford Worcester & Wolverhampton Railway, the main line company which would, ultimately, assume responsibility for the Stratford & Moreton Railway.

TYPE OF ORIGINAL RAIL USED ON THE STRATFORD AND MORETON TRAMROAD.

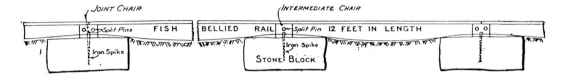

Details of the method of laying permanent way in the tramway era. It will be noted that the Bledlington iron rails were laid with their flanges uppermost. Joints were effected by 'joint chairs' rather than fishplates.

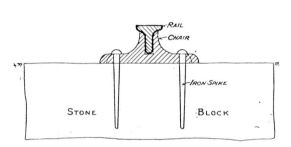

Sectional View of Rail Joint.

CHAPTER TWO

THE OXFORD WORCESTER &
WOLVERHAMPTON RAILWAY PERIOD
(1847-1863)

THE tramway worked fairly successfully through out the 1830s and early 1840s, but the threat of direct railway competition remained, and this threat assumed tangible form in the early 1840s when the Oxford Worcester & Wolverhampton Railway Company was formed to build a main line from Oxford, through Moreton and Worcester, to Wolverhampton. Promoted by Black Country coal owners and industrialists, the OW & WR was initially seen as a full member of the Great Western 'family', and with Isambard Kingdom Brunel as its Engineer this new main line was to be a broad gauge route.

The Great Western was, in many ways, an ideal ally for the Oxford Worcester & Wolverhampton, and the Worcester company's promoters, in presenting their scheme to the investing public, were able to suggest that the new line, when built, would become a major broad gauge trunk route between London and the West Midlands.

THE OXFORD WORCESTER & WOLVERHAMPTON RAILWAY IS FORMED

At a public meeting held in the Guildhall at Worcester – one of the many called to discuss the projected railway – Francis Rufford, a Stourbridge banker who was to become chairman of the OW & WR, declared that by adopting the Great Western broad gauge of 7ft 0¼in, the Worcester line would gain untold advantages, not only because of the increased speeds made possible by the wider gauge, but also because of the bigger loads that could be carried in broad gauge vehicles. Rufford went on to say that, although they were independent of the Great Western Railway, 'they had, in their dealings with that company, received from them the most courteous treatment; and in future proceedings should act only in connection with them, and in confirmation with their advice and recommendations'. Other speakers referred to the dangerous monopoly enjoyed by rival companies such as the London & Birmingham, and finally, on a lighter note, Michael Glazebrook, a Stourbridge glass manufacturer who was soon to emerge as an active member of the OW & WR board, stated that he sent £250,000 worth of glass by rail each year, and the narrow gauge companies broke 1½ per cent more than the GWR!

With enthusiastic support from West Midlands manufacturers, and the backing of the Great Western Railway, the Oxford Worcester & Wolverhampton Bill was presented to Parliament in the early months of 1845, together with a related Bill for a northwards extension of the broad gauge from Oxford to Rugby. Both lines would diverge from the existing railhead at Oxford, the OW & WR heading north west to Worcester via Moreton-in-Marsh and Evesham, and the Oxford & Rugby striking due north towards Banbury.

Although at first glance the idea of two broad gauge main lines may have been somewhat extravagant, the Great Western plans were quite logical. The Worcester line, which would connect with the Grand Junction Railway at Wolverhampton, would enable goods and passengers from the GWR to reach the west coast main line to Scotland, whereas the Oxford & Rugby would provide a useful connection with the Midland Counties system at Rugby.

The two Great Western Bills passed through Parliament at a time in which there was immense concern over the evils of the 'break of gauge', and certain radical politicians were known to favour state intervention to ensure eventual uniformity of gauge. The Bills were, as a result, subjected to unprecedented scrutiny, but in spite of bitter opposition from the London & Birmingham Railway, the Midland Railway, and individual politicians such as Richard Cobden, the Oxford & Rugby and the Oxford Worcester & Wolverhampton Bills both received the Royal Assent on 4th August 1845.

The Oxford Worcester & Wolverhampton Railway Act (8 & 9 Vic. cap. 184) provided consent for the construction of a railway from the Oxford branch of the GWR, through Evesham and Worcester, to the Grand Junction station at Wolverhampton, with branches to the River Severn at Diglis Basin, to the Birmingham & Gloucester Railway at Stoke Prior, from Amblecote to Stourbridge, and from Brettel Lane to Kingswinford. The Act stipulated that the OW & WR was to be 'constructed and completed in all respects to the satisfaction of the engineer for the time being to the Great Western Railway', and be 'formed of such a gauge, and according to such mode of construction as will admit of the same being worked continuously with the said Great Western Railway'. The Great Western was empowered to complete the line, should the OW & WR fail to do so, and six of the sixteen Oxford Worcester & Wolverhampton directors were to be Great Western nominees. A further section of the Act empowered the OW & WR to take a permanent lease of the Stratford & Moreton Railway at an agreed rent.

In August 1846 Brunel reported that work had started at various points on the 89 mile OW & WR route, and by the beginning of 1847 over 2,800 navvies were at work on the new main line. It seemed that the Oxford Worcester & Wolverhampton Railway was destined for success, but, sadly, all progress was halted by a terrible economic crisis which hit world trading in the 1840s. After several wet summers, the corn and potato crops failed, causing starvation in many rural areas and throwing the Victorian banking system into total chaos. In 1848 much of Europe was paralysed by a series of revolutions, and against this background of continuing crisis, the OW & WR found itself in serious financial difficulties.

By the end of the year all construction work was at a standstill.

The OW & WR directors appealed to the Great Western for help, but the latter company was itself suffering during the prevailing trade depression, and could do little to help its former protégé.

However, the Great Western seemed to be hurrying on with the completion of a rival main line between Banbury, Birmingham and Wolverhampton, and the OW & WR, viewing this as a breach of faith, broke away from its former GWR allegiance and formed a new alliance with the rival London & North Western Railway. An agreement, signed on 21st February 1851, opened the way for completion of the OW & WR as a standard gauge line, worked with the aid of L & NWR locomotives and rolling stock; one result of this unexpected alliance was the eventual resignation of Brunel as OW & WR Engineer on 17th March 1852.

Meanwhile, the Stratford & Moreton Railway had continued to function more or less undisturbed by these momentous events. The line had, since May 1847, been rented by the OW & WR, and all receipts from 'tonnages, weighings, wharfage, rents, licences for passengers, sand fines, etc.' now passed directly to the Worcester company. In fact, until October 1850 (when the first section of the OW & WR was opened to traffic) the horse tramway was one of the Oxford Worcester & Wolverhampton Railway's few sources of income.

In addition to its renting of the tramway, the OW & WR also secured control of the 25 mile long Stratford Canal. This was worked as a sort of detached branch line, and like the tramway it provided a welcome source of income at a time when the OW & WR proper was still under construction.

Oxford Worcester & Wolverhampton directors' reports provide many interesting glimpses of the Stratford & Moreton Railway in operation. It was usual during the late 1840s and early 1850s for the tramway to be mentioned in OW & WR half-yearly reports, and the report for the six months ending on 30th June 1849 contained the following note:

'On the Stratford & Moreton Railway the receipts had been £1,295 0s 1d, and the expenditure, including fixed rent for the same, £1,702 10s 4d, leaving a balance against the company of £407 9s 4d.'

Six months later, the receipts for the half-year ending 31st December 1849 had been £1,751 18s 4d, while expenditure, excluding rent, totalled £473 11s 3d. (A full analysis of income and expenditure for the half year under review is given in *Table 2*).

The Oxford Worcester & Wolverhampton main line was still, as yet, unfinished, although in September 1849 the long-suffering OW & WR shareholders were told that from Tipton to Dudley the line was 'practically completed and ready to receive the permanent way'. From Dudley to Stourbridge, a distance of about four miles, very little had been accomplished, but south of Stourbridge the sections of line between Droitwich and Worcester, Droitwich and Stoke Prior, and from Worcester to Pershore were 'nearly ready to receive the permanent way'. From Pershore towards Shipton-under-Wychwood the works were in a forward state, but the southernmost extremity of the line was the least advanced.

On 5th October 1850 a single line between Abbots Wood Junction on the Midland line and a temporary station at Shrub Hill was brought into use, but with Campden Tunnel, to the north of Moreton-in-Marsh, still unfinished there seemed little possibility of an early opening of the main line to Oxford. There was, nevertheless, a possibility that the Stratford & Moreton Railway could be physically linked to the OW & WR at Moreton-in-Marsh, where the new railway would cut through the tramway terminus, thereby providing a ready-made branch to Stratford; the Oxford Worcester & Wolverhampton directors therefore sent Brunel to survey the twenty-year-old horse tramway with a view to incorporating it in the company's system.

Not surprisingly, the meticulous, half-French engineer found much to criticise; the line was still laid with fish-bellied iron rails secured to stone blocks, and its civil engineering was 'poor' with 'small clearances and poor drainage'. Brunel's most scathing comments concerned the gauge which, he claimed, 'varied between 4ft 8½ins and 4ft 9ins'. Brunel considered that steam locomotives could be used, at least on the southern part of the route, but considerable expenditure would be necessary in order to bring the line up to modern standards. Undeterred, the OW & WR directors decided to proceed with a programme of track renewal, albeit to a standard below that suggested by their engineer.

TABLE 2:   Income & Expenditure for the half-year ending 31st December 1849

Income				*Expenditure*			
Tonnages	£1,620	9s	11d	Repairs and materials	£135	15s	7d
Weighings	£57	4s	11d	Salaries	£277	15s	8d
Wharfage	£4	12s	7d	Rent to be paid	£13	13s	7d
Rents to be received	£26	16s	6d	General expenses	£17	18s	11d
Licences for passengers	£33	1s	0d	Taxes & rates	£13	15s	1d
Sand fines	£9	13s	5d	Stationery	£14	17s	5d
				Fixed rent (6 months)	£1268	15s	0d
				Profits for half year	£9	8s	1d
	£1751	18s	4d		£1751	18s	4d

The prospect of an upgraded Stratford & Moreton Railway seems to have excited considerable interest in OW & WR circles, and at the half-year meeting held in August 1852 Michael Grazebrook (in the chair) announced that the S & MR was 'proceeding satisfactorily and promised to be a good source of traffic' when the Worcester to Oxford main line was in operation. The OW & WR directors were so pleased with the line that their half-yearly report contained a special mention:

'The Stratford & Moreton was managed by its own former officers up to Christmas last. Since that period your directors have, by a committee of their board, superintended the working. The result during the half-year has been that, notwithstanding the permanent way has been much improved, and consequently a more than ordinary expenditure has been incurred, the expenditure has exceeded the income by £123 10s 9d, whereas in the corresponding half-year of 1851 the expenditure over income was £400 19s 9d; in the same period of 1850 was £331 15s 8d; in the same period of 1849 was £378 11s 4d; and in the same period of 1848 was £580 8s 3d.

'Your directors think that this is a satisfactory result, and trust so soon as the line is opened between this railway at Moreton and Oxford, not only will its income exceed its expenditure, but it will be a valuable feeder to the main line'.

The OW & WR was opened from Stourbridge to Evesham on 1st May 1852, and in the previous month the company had asked John Fowler (who had replaced Brunel as engineer) to lay longitudinal timber sleepers on the remaining section between Evesham, Moreton and Wolvercot Junction. Curiously, the engineer was instructed to lay a 'single, mixed gauge line' with the proviso that 'the iron rails be laid in the first instance *on the broad gauge only*'. With this work under way, the tramway was closed to all traffic in the early months of 1853 so that OW & WR engineers could carry out certain modifications; the work was described as follows by the Oxford Worcester & Wolverhampton directors in their report for the six months ending 30th June 1853:

'Stratford & Moreton – During the past half-year this tramway was closed for some weeks, and a considerable outlay was incurred in order to adapt it to the passage of carriages for passenger traffic between the main line and the towns of Stratford and Shipston, and also for the wagons and trucks of the gauge of the main line. The closing of the tramway has materially diminished the half-year receipts; and the expenses upon the works the directors have carried to capital as permanent alterations. The traffic is now increasing, and as soon as the works in progress at Moreton, connecting the tramway to the main line, are complete, a considerable improvement in the receipts may be expected.'

A REGAUGING?

The intriguing reference to adapting the tramway 'to the gauge of the main line' has led some secondary sources to suggest that its gauge was altered from 4ft to 4ft 8½ins during the spring of 1853. However, Brunel's report clearly states that the line was laid to the standard gauge of 4ft 8½ins (albeit with distortions resulting from lack of maintenance) and this would seem to prove that it was a standard gauge line from its inception, and was *not* widened in 1853. The poor condition of much of the trackwork meant that the line needed regauging in places where the rails had spread simply to

ensure conformity of gauge, and this may be the explanation for the mysterious 'regauging'.

Less plausibly, it is possible that the OW & WR directors, having told their engineer to lay the Oxford main line with 7ft gauge track, intended adapting the tramway to accept *broad gauge* wagons. Although this may appear somewhat far-fetched, it is known that, prior to their disagreement with the GWR, the OW & WR directors had considered laying a mixed gauge line along the route of the Stratford Canal. If implemented, this canal-to-railway conversion would have provided a convenient main line between Lapworth and Birmingham, which could, at a later date be transferred to the GWR. In the event, the furious row which developed between the OW & WR and its patron ensured that the Oxford Worcester & Wolverhampton Railway was opened as a purely standard gauge line, and the Stratford Canal remained in use as a waterway.

OPERATING THE TRAMWAY IN THE OW & WR PERIOD

It seems that the tramway was fully operational when the OW & WR main line was opened from Evesham to Wolvercot Junction on 4th June 1853, and in the next few years the line was shown in *Bradshaw* as a branch of the Oxford to Worcester line with two 'trains' daily, running from Stratford-upon-Avon to Moreton in connection with the main line.

The line was still horse-operated, and the service was accordingly slow. The first up working left Stratford at 6.15am, reaching Shipston by 7.00am. After reversal, the single horse-drawn vehicle continued southwards to Moreton in time for travellers to catch the 8.35am train to Oxford. In the down direction, there was a departure from Moreton at 9.45am which reached Shipston at 10.55am and Stratford by 11.45am. An afternoon service departed from Stratford at 4.15pm reaching Moreton two hours later. Finally, the balancing down working left Moreton at 6.20pm. One assumes that the long gap between the morning and afternoon passenger services allowed goods services to be run as required. Through tickets were available for passengers wishing to travel through to Oxford or other destinations, typical fares being (from Stratford to Oxford) 8/- first class, 6/- second class and 4/- third class.

The fact that provision was made for three classes of travel adds substance to the legend that an old OW & WR 4-wheeled composite carriage was used on the line. One theory suggests that third class travellers were treated as 'outside' passengers on a stage coach and rode on the roof! The timetable in operation around 1858 is reproduced overleaf.

In general, receipts from the tramway over the next few years averaged £3,000 pa, but this was hardly sufficient to cover the rent of £2,360 for the main line and £177 10s for the Shipston branch which the OW & WR had agreed to pay. On the other hand, operating expenses were few as all services were provided by private traders –

STRATFORD & MORETON RAILWAY: 1858 TIMETABLE						
Moreton Junction	9.45am	6.20pm		Stratford-upon-Avon	6.15am	4.15pm
Shipston-on-Stour	10.55am	7.30pm		Shipston-on-Stour	7.00am	5.00pm
Stratford-upon-Avon	11.45am	8.20pm		Moreton Junction	8.15am	6.15pm

NB The times shown at 'Moreton Junction' in *Bradshaw* refer to connecting main line services rather than tramway arrivals or departures, but in the table Moreton timings have been adjusted to show actual S & M times. (A 2-hour journey time has been assumed.)

the passenger service, for example, was operated by a Mr Bull of the George Hotel, Shipston.

It is likely that once connections were available at Moreton the tramway enjoyed something of a renaissance, and its appearance in *Bradshaw* must have contributed to a modest increase in passenger traffic. It is easy to imagine Mr Bull's horse-drawn vehicle ambling through the countryside filled with parcels, crates, market produce and chattering villagers. One small problem at this time concerned the junction at Ilmington, which faced towards Stratford rather than Moreton, and travellers intending to reach Shipston from Moreton were faced with a reversal before they could reach their destination. Those travelling between Shipston and Stratford, on the other hand, could travel direct, though in view of the slow speeds involved this was perhaps no real advantage.

One beneficial result of the OW & WR takeover was that, with more money available for maintenance, the trackwork was improved. This may have allowed a small increase in speed, and in this context it is interesting to note the way in which S & M horses would be detached from their wagons at the start of falling gradients and then mount small platforms which extended from the rear of passenger vehicles. Alternatively, an empty wagon could be coupled to the rear of goods trains especially for the horse, who would no doubt look forward to a rest when he came to a descending gradient and trot to the rear of his train with very little encouragement!

In a well-publicised experiment, carried out on the Surrey Iron Railway as the result of a wager, a single horse once pulled a twelve-wagon stone train, weighing 38½ tons, for six miles. Moreover, contemporary prints often show *trains* of wagons on other early 19th century horse-worked tramways, and in view of this it seems likely that similar trains were run on the Stratford & Moreton line. It is estimated that horses could typically pull loads of about 8 tons on iron rails (as opposed to just 2 tons on macadam roads) and on this basis, two or more of the tramway's small wagons could easily have been hauled by one horse.

The situation regarding heavier, main line rolling stock is less clear cut, but on balance it is likely that when OW & WR wagons were sent on to the tramway they were pulled by just one animal. One assumes that, in this case, portable shafts were attached to the buffers or side chains of main line vehicles, and that a man would walk beside the wagons to operate their brakes on falling gradients. When horses were used for shunting purposes on Victorian railways they often walked on specially provided 'tow paths' beside the railway lines. This facility was not provided on the horse tramway,

and horses therefore walked in front of their trains, with consequent danger in the event of an uncontrolled descent.

There is a persistent legend that steam power was occasionally used on the tramway. William James had certainly envisaged the use of locomotives on both his Bishop's Stortford and Stratford & Moreton lines (and in later years he was an enthusiastic supporter of the Liverpool & Manchester line). The use of locomotives at some future date was clearly implicit in James's choice of Bledlington rails, but, even if he had not gone bankrupt, it is unlikely that James could have transported a locomotive to Stratford. The physical problems involved in moving locomotives from the industrial areas of northern England where they were made was immense, the only practicable way being by sea and thence by river (this was how the first GWR locomotive reached West Drayton in November 1837). However, the cost of transporting a locomotive, say from Newcastle to Stratford via the River Avon, would have made the introduction of steam power an uneconomic proposition until the Stratford & Moreton was connected to the OW & WR at Moreton-in-Marsh. There was then nothing to stop an engine running through to Shipston or even Stratford-upon-Avon, and the Oxford Worcester & Wolverhampton Railway had one or two small locomotives which might have ventured onto the tramway without seriously damaging its track. These included two diminutive 0-4-2Ts, which had been built by the Railway Foundry, Leeds, in 1853; numbered 35 and 36 in the OW & WR fleet, their driving wheels were only 3ft 5ins in diameter, and their cylinders measured just 9¼in x 14in. Such tiny engines would, one feels, have been ideally suited for use on the tramway, though sadly, there is no way of discovering if they ever ran on the line.

The tramway was at this time still laid with fish-bellied iron rails, though it seems that at least some conventional bullhead track had been laid. In 1856 John Fowler inspected the entire OW & WR system in compliance with a request made by the directors, and his report is worth quoting in detail as it suggests that the tramway had been completely relaid in 1853:

'The permanent way of the main line of the Oxford Worcester & Wolverhampton consists entirely of bridge rails and longitudinal timbers. The rails are partly 70lbs and partly 60lbs to the yard. The Chipping Norton branch is laid with cross sleepers and 60lb double-headed rails and ordinary chairs. The Stratford & Moreton Tramway is laid in a similar manner to the Chipping Norton branch, but with rails and timber much lighter.'

Taken at face value, Fowler's report would seem to prove conclusively that the tramway was laid with bullhead rail on cross sleepers, but when Daniel Gooch visited the line at Stratford-upon-Avon in 1867 he was surprised to find fish-bellied rails *in situ*. Gooch had been born at Bledlington in 1816, and he clearly remembered George Stephenson, Joseph Locke and other famous personalities coming to the iron-works (where his father was manager) to see John Birkenshaw's revolutionary new rails. In view of this he took a great interest in the tramway's rails and asked for a sample to be sent to him 'as a relic of the early days of railways'. Making further enquiries, he 'learned from Mr Greaves whose father was interested in laying the road, that the . . . rails were those originally obtained in 1830'.

Gooch's diary would seem to contradict Fowler's report, suggesting that the OW & WR engineer did not inspect the tramway very thoroughly. It is possible, however, that Fowler inspected Moreton-in-Marsh station and the southern extremity of the tramway, and failed to examine the rest of the system. The newly-laid connections at Moreton probably *were* laid with bullhead rail on cross sleepers, but as Gooch and all later visitors refer to 'fish-bellied rail' it seems that the rest of the line was laid, in the main, with its original pre-OW & WR rails and stone sleepers.

Responsibility for the S & M Railway during the OW & WR period rested with Mr A. C. Sherriff, the OW & WR General Manager. Formerly employed by the North Eastern Railway, Mr Sherriff had been appointed in 1856, the OW & WR board hoping that this experienced officer would be able to inject some new life into their poverty-stricken railway. The new General Manager was intrigued by the tramway, and suggested that revenue might be increased if passengers were conveyed in an ordinary carriage. He also wished to see the line for himself, and in late August 1857 he ventured onto the line with an engine, the only time in which a locomotive is known to have worked over the line prior to the 1880s. The event attracted much attention locally, and on 5th September 1857 *The Worcester Herald* printed the following brief report:

'A few days since the inhabitants of Shipston-on-Stour were greatly surprised at the unexpected arrival of a locomotive engine, an event long looked for by many of the tradespeople. Mr Sherriff came with the engine for the purpose of inspecting the line from Moreton, distant about ten miles.'

On another occasion, Mr Sherriff inspected the entire route of the line, taking with him his assistant Robert Hudson. The journey was made by ordinary passenger service, and was later recalled with affection by Hudson (who was destined to work at Stratford for many years, assuming local responsibility for both the S & M Railway and the rail-way-owned Stratford-upon-Avon Canal). Although Hudson's description of his first journey to Stratford has been published elsewhere, it is worth repeating in so far as it represents an important, first-hand description of the line by a responsible OW & WR employee. There may, in places, be small exaggerations, but Hudson's narrative would seem to prove that S & M horses did indeed ride downhill on

falling gradients. The following passage first appeared in *London Society* in May 1864 as part of a feature on the Shakespeare Tercentenary celebrations:

'Of all those who by road or rail, afoot or mounted, will go pilgrimaging to the Poet's land, it is not probable that anyone will reach Stratford by the mode of transit which first conveyed the writer there: for Stratford at that time had no railway – or, at least, if it had one, the people of Stratford refused to call it anything but a tramway. And by this tram from the village of Moreton-in-Marsh, some fifteen miles away, the present writer first made his way to the Shakespearian shrine. His recollections of that ride are a curious combination of the impressions made by travelling by coach and travelling by rail.

'The journey was performed outside an ordinary railway carriage, which had been adapted to the necessities of horse traction. It was fitted with a box for the driver, and seats beside him for passengers. Attached to the carriage in front was a platform, on which the sagacious horse (the only locomotive used on the Stratford & Moreton Railway) mounted when it had drawn our carriage to the top of an incline, thus escaping being tripped up as we descended at a rattling good speed. The Inspectors of the Board of Trade not having discovered this tramway, the occurrence or non-occurrence of accidents was left chiefly to the goodness of Providence. When we came to the foot of the incline, the guard applied his brake as tightly as he could; we all, to the best of our individual capacities, held on to our seats, and, if we had taken firm hold, we thus managed to avoid being pitched off head-foremost. When the carriage came to a stand, the horse dismounted and drew us along as before.

'There was a tunnel, too, on approaching which the driver was kind enough to suggest that such of the outside passengers as thought it likely they would have further use for their brains, should duck their heads as low as possible, and carry their hats in their hands.

'And thus following chiefly the course of the river Stour, we wound very pleasantly through shady lanes, where the high hedgerows, forming a grateful screen from the hot sun, could be reached by the hand on either side. Or we ran along the public highway, not separated from it by any fence, stopping now and then to take up or set down a wayfarer, or to refresh our thirsty selves with beer.

'At what pace we went, or whether that pace would be most approximately calculated in miles to the hour or hours to the mile, we hardly know. It was all very pleasant, and seemed to last so long – we were of the opinion that, except on the break-neck inclines, no great despatch was either sought after or obtained, and it would generally have been quite safe to get down and walk a little.

'There was always pleasant matter for speculation, too, as to what county we were in at that particular moment. For, starting in Gloucestershire, we found ourselves presently in Worcestershire, forth-with in Warwickshire, then for another breathing space in Worcester-shire, anon again in Gloucestershire, back into Worcestershire, then once more into Gloucestershire, until at last, the graceful spire of Stratford rising before us, we trundled across the beautiful Avon, and ended our journey in Warwickshire – the shires in these parts being intermixed very singularly, and we having in our short journey made no less than seven changes of this kind.

'Since then we have visited Stratford many scores of times, having, in fact, come to be almost a townsman of that place, but never again have we journeyed, nor shall we journey, there so pleasantly. The tramway, it is true, still exists, and is worthy the attention of all archaeologists; but passengers to Stratford no longer pass over its ancient, perilous rails. It exists only as a superseded idea. Its modest glories have paled before those of the modern and quite uninteresting railways which have pierced Stratford from the north and from the south.'

DECLINE OF THE TRAMWAY

On 12th July 1859 the OW & WR opened a 9¼ mile branch from Honeybourne to Stratford-upon-Avon, and this new railway effectively killed the northern extremity of the tramway. Death, however, was protracted, and when Gooch visited the line some eight years later he found it still in operation with the 'rails . . . in good order'. It is true that Moreton to Stratford-upon-Avon services did not appear in *Bradshaws Timetables* after 1859, but this does not necessarily mean that all passenger services ceased.

Goods traffic certainly continued, both to Shipston and along the main line to Stratford, and as far as Shipston was concerned, the tramway continued to play an important part in the local transport system; in pre-railway days the little town had profited from passing traffic on the busy Oxford to Stratford turnpike, and inn keepers, stablemen and shopkeepers all earned their livings by catering for road travellers. With the spread of the railways elsewhere in the country, this source of income evaporated, leaving Shipston dangerously isolated and under these circumstances, local traders valued the tramway as their one link with the outside world, fearing that its closure would ruin their business.

The tramway had never been really profitable, and as early as 1856 it was said to be losing £1,600 a year. This figure was of course a general figure for the whole line, and it seems that, if taken in isolation, the Shipston branch was marginally profitable. Nevertheless, the OW & WR continued to treat the Stratford & Moreton Railway as a single entity, allowing the entire system to run down.

In an effort to reduce expenditure, maintenance was kept to the minimum required to permit the passage of traffic, and in time the iron spikes used to secure the chairs to their sleepers tended to work loose – a result of the holes drilled in the stone blocks becoming hopelessly enlarged. In an attempt to repair the track without the expense of new equipment, passing loops and sidings were lifted to provide spare parts (thereby reducing line capacity to the detriment of services). In spite of this remedial action, derailments became increasingly common, particularly when heavy main line vehicles were brought onto the tramway.

THE LAST DAYS OF THE OW & WR

The Oxford Worcester & Wolverhampton Railway – itself a somewhat happy-go-lucky concern – was unlikely to close the tramway, but in 1858 a series of events in the long-running war between the OW & WR and the Great Western ensured that sooner or later the tramway would pass into GWR hands. By 1858 the OW & WR had become an extensive system in its own right, with 168 miles of line in operation or under construction. In that year, the company decided to join forces with the Newport, Abergavenny & Hereford Railway in order to build a line between Worcester and Hereford. Unfortunately, the Newport, Abergavenny and Hereford was in such parlous financial straits that it could not survive as an independent company and complete its expensive extensions. The NA & HR directors therefore agreed to amalgamate their undertaking with the Worcester & Hereford and Oxford Worcester & Wolverhampton Railways, and a new company, known as the West Midland

Railway, was created by an Act of Parliament obtained on 1st July 1860. Inevitably, this new organisation, being much larger than the original OW & WR, was less tolerant towards unprofitable subsidiaries such as the Stratford & Moreton Railway.

Meanwhile, relations between Worcester and Paddington had definitely improved. The quarrel between the OW & WR and its parent had always been linked to the gauge question, but in February 1858 the GWR, by then a narrow gauge as well as a broad gauge railway, agreed to release the Worcester company from its obligation to provide broad gauge facilities. Furthermore, there had always been pro-Great Western directors on the OW & WR board, and as these individuals gradually assumed positions of influence, the hostility that had once existed between the estranged companies began to subside. Finally, in the summer of 1861 it was announced that the West Midland and Great Western companies would amalgamate.

The revolt of the OW & WR was at last at an end, and as an interim measure the Great Western undertook to lease as much of the WMR as it could, and was granted full running powers over the rest. A full amalgamation followed on 1st August 1863, and thus the Stratford & Moreton tramway became an unwanted appendage of the Great Western Railway.

CLOSURE PROPOSALS

Stratford-upon-Avon was, at this time, served by no less than three railways. The OW & WR branch, opened in 1859, had been joined on 10th October 1860 by the GW-worked Stratford-upon-Avon Railway, but these two lines did not at first connect, the OW & WR terminus being in Sanctuary Lane (later Sanctus Street) while the GWR's mixed-gauge line terminated at Birmingham Road on the opposite side of the town. A short connecting line was brought into use on 24th July 1861, and on 1st January 1863 a new station was opened in Alcester Road roughly mid-way between the Stratford-upon-Avon and OW & WR stations, both of which were then closed.

The Stratford & Moreton – antiquated, poorly-maintained, and unconnected to the other lines in Stratford – was clearly surplus to requirements, and in 1862 the West Midland Railway (already in effect part of the GWR system) announced that the tramway would be closed.

The closure proposals brought forth a storm of protest, and in what must surely have been one of the first 'Save our Railway' campaigns in history, the inhabitants of Shipston-on-Stour and the surrounding area called a public meeting in the George Hotel. This meeting was chaired by H. J. Sheldon of Brailes, and attended by many influential landowners from the surrounding area. Speakers lamented the way in which the town had stagnated since the withdrawal of its stage coaches, and complained that while other localities 'were well supplied with railway accommodation', Shipston was 'entirely isolated'. There were, however, tentative proposals for a new 'line of railway from Banbury, by Tadmarton, Traitorsford, Mitford Bridge, skirting Shipston and Ilmington, to Honeybourne or Evesham'. Such a line, the meeting was told, would prove 'of incalculable service to the district through which it passed, and would form a direct communication with South Wales'. This new route had been surveyed, and the landowners through whose land it would pass were said to be favourably disposed to the scheme.

The meeting decided that any new railway would be an advantage to Shipston, and perhaps unwittingly, the local protesters thereby saved their tramway. Faced with determined opposition, not only from humble traders but also from major landowners, the West Midland and Great Western companies decided to retain the Stratford & Moreton Railway in its entirety, thereby making possible an eventual revival of part of the route as a steam-worked branch line some two decades later.

The Great Western had been swayed, not by the arguments against closure, but by the nightmare prospect of some rival company establishing itself in the immediate vicinity; if the S & M tramway was allowed to close there was every chance that another railway would fill the vacuum. It made sense, therefore, for the GWR to keep the horse line in being.

The tramway, meanwhile, continued to serve the district between Moreton and Stratford, and the pages of local newspapers such as The Worcester Herald and The Oxford Journal provide occasional glimpses of the line in everyday operation at that time. On 5th July 1862, for instance, The Worcester Herald reported an accident had recently taken place between Moreton and Shipston when a young man named Robert Cook, an employee of Mr Bull, was killed by a wagon. He had been travelling from Shipston 'in company with his brother with an empty truck drawn by three horses' but fell from the wooden buffers at the front of the wagon and was crushed as the vehicle passed over him.

Accidents were, it seems, fairly common occurrences – a result of excessive speed when descending gradients, which in turn, may have resulted from widespread drinking on the part of the line's drivers. On one occasion a tramp fell asleep on the track near Alscot Park and had his legs crushed by a passing wagon, while in another accident a driver fell off and was killed by his own vehicle.

Petty crime was not unknown, and on 21st July 1866 The Worcester Herald reported the case of John Sabin and Henry Parker – two small boys caught stealing grease 'from the wheels of trucks on the Great Western tramroad'. Happily, the bench decided not to inflict any punishment; instead the magistrates imposed a primitive form of probation, leaving the malefactors 'to be called upon at any time for punishment'. On a footnote, it is worth noting that the 'trucks' involved in this incident must have been ordinary railway vehicles, with grease-filled axle boxes – and this indicated that, as early as the 1860s, GWR goods stock worked through from Moreton to Shipston or beyond.

Other minor transgressions related to the line's own rules and regulations, and it is interesting to note that tramway officials were not averse to taking legal action against wrongdoers. On 21st March 1873 for example, The Stratford-upon-Avon Herald reported the case of two drivers who had been summoned by the Shipston-on-Stour tramway clerk for what was in effect a parking offence:

'Richard Caudell and Joseph Giles, both of Shipston, were summoned by Charles Mace for having on the 17th instant obstructed the free passage of the tramway from Moreton to Shipston by placing thereon a wagon laden with coals contrary to the regulations of the Great Western company made April 10th 1867, whereby they had incurred a penalty of £5. Mr Hudson represented the company and called evidence to show that on the day in question the defendants were the drivers of a wagon laden with coals, belonging to James Bartlett, which they should have brought and placed on the Shipston wharf, instead of which they left it on the rails in a dangerous part of the road and had it not been seen and removed, great danger might have occurred from the obstruction. Defendants did not appear and as Mr Hudson stated that the company did not press for a severe penalty, they were fined 21s each, including costs, in default of 14 days hard labour.'

Little is known of the ordinary tramway drivers, though in later years Frank Hathaway, a retired baker living at Ilmington, was able to recall his grandfather, George Hathaway who had been a driver on the line. Mr Hathaway was a local carrier who had owned his own tramway wagons, using them in pairs. Known locally as 'Monkey boxes', these vehicles carried both passengers and freight, a regular source of traffic being fruit and vegetables from the Stour Valley, some of which was grown by Mr Hathaway himself. On arrival at Stratford, the produce was sold to regular wholesalers and then sent to Birmingham via Hatton and the GWR main line.

Frank Hathaway remembered that his grandfather's wagons were covered by a simple, tent-like structure, resembling the sheeted hold of a canal boat and supported in much the same way by triangular 'cratches' affixed to either end of the vehicles. A horizontal plank provided support for canvas sheets which, in wet weather, were let down to protect passengers and freight. Interestingly, George Hathaway's pairs of wagons were apparently accompanied by a flat wagon which was used by the horse when descending gradients. Sadly, old Mr Hathaway's long career as a driver came to an abrupt end when he was involved in an accident on the tramway. He died later in Moreton-in-the-Marsh, the first fatality in the town's new Cottage Hospital.

Another tramway driver, remembered only dimly by elderly Shipston residents, was Bill Sanders (or Saunders?) who, like George Hathaway, was a self-employed carrier. It seems that Mr Sanders also died as the result of an accident on the tramway, and it is perhaps worth reflecting that this unregulated, horse-operated railway, with its decrepit equipment and happy-go-lucky drivers, was not, by any stretch of the imagination, the safest means of transport between Stratford and Moreton.

Moreton-in-Marsh, looking north along the present A429 (the Fosse Way) in July 1930, and showing the gothic-style Redesdale Hall. The White Hart Hotel on the extreme right was once a busy coaching inn.

National Railway Museum

CHAPTER THREE

A WORCESTERSHIRE BRANCH LINE
(1863-1914)

IN June 1864, a small company calling itself the East & West Junction Railway, obtained Parliamentary consent for a 33¼ mile branch from Stratford-upon-Avon to Greens Norton. Leaving the Great Western Stratford branch at Old Stratford, the authorised route diverged south eastwards, crossing first the River Avon, and then the Stratford & Moreton Railway, before heading due east to its destination. At Greens Norton, a junction with the Northampton & Banbury Junction line would provide a link to the London & North Western Railway at Blisworth.

After many vicissitudes, the East & West Junction was opened between Kineton and Fenny Compton on 1st June 1871, and completed throughout from Stratford to Greens Norton on 1st July 1873. This new line passed beneath the Stratford & Moreton Railway at a point later known as 'Clifford Siding', an iron girder bridge being provided for the benefit of tramway users. In theory, the East & West Junction should have developed as a useful cross-country link between the GWR and L & NWR systems, but sadly, its traffic failed to materialise and by January 1875 the little company was in the hands of the receiver.

A MIDLAND INCURSION?

The Great Western probably viewed its tiny neighbour with a mixture of pity and amusement, but in retrospect, it seems likely that the opening of the unfortunate East & West Junction Railway may have led, ultimately, to the revival of the Shipston-on-Stour line as a conventional steam-operated branch. Harmless in itself, the East & West Junction soon attracted attention from the London & North Western, Midland and other ambitious main line companies. The Great Western viewed this situation with some trepidation, remembering how, in the 1860s, the Midland had encouraged the formation of various locally-based (but highly ambitious) cross-country schemes. In 1865, for example, there were proposals for a line running from Banbury to Blockley, and in the following year powers were obtained for an extension towards South Wales. At the same time, the Midland was covertly supporting the 'East Gloucestershire Railway', which hoped to extend the Witney branch westwards to join existing Midland lines in Cheltenham.

The proposed line from Banbury to Blockley was of special significance in relation to Shipston-on-Stour in so far as it would have placed the town on a main line from the East Midlands to South Wales, and if this ambitious scheme had been completed it would obviously have altered the local railway system out of all recognition. Furthermore, the Blockley scheme was championed by Henry James Sheldon of Brailes House, who was particularly keen to see improved transport links in the Shipston-on-Stour area. As we have seen, Henry Sheldon had chaired an influential meeting held in Shipston in May 1865, and those in attendance had enthusiastically supported the South Wales line.

It should be stressed that in 1865, the proposed Banbury to South Wales line seemed destined for success. In that year, the scheme's supporters obtained two Acts (28 & 29 Vic. cap. 361 and 28 & 29 Vic. cap. 362) which authorised extensions of the Northampton & Banbury Junction Railway and empowered the N & BJR promoters to raise no less than £645,000 in shares and £211,500 by loans, while in the following year the company obtained further powers which raised its combined share and loan capital to almost £2,000,000. Significantly the 1866 Act also granted running powers over a section of the Midland Railway between Bickford and Tewkesbury, over the Ross & Monmouth Railway, and over the Dean Forest & Monmouth Railway between Newport and Monmouth.

Behind these grandiose schemes was the Midland's desire to reach the South Wales coal fields, but there was, at the same time, a degree of popular support for the new main line in towns and villages such as Shipston. On 12th August 1865, for example, *The Railway Times* reported a half-yearly meeting of the Northampton & Banbury Junction Railway at which Henry Sheldon, now an N & BJR director, spoke persuasively of the need for better railway facilities:

> 'Mr H. L. Sheldon (a director) . . . said that he resided between Banbury and Blockley, and was well acquainted with the wants of the locality, and could bear evidence to the great requirement there had been ever since he could remember for additional means of communication throughout the district. It was a thickly populated agricultural country and grazing district, from which many thousand head of cattle might be conveyed to the metropolis if proper communication were afforded. The line would also be a great benefit to the inhabitants of the district, by giving them coal at a much less cost, which, under the present disadvantages of carriage – having it to be carted a distance of ten miles – raised the price to a frightful extent, and which, indeed, almost precluded the use of it to the poorer classes. He was sure the projected line would secure not only a great local but a great through traffic.'

The prospect of a new, competitive route to the South Wales coal field was anathema to the Great Western, but when, in May 1866, the failure of bankers Overend & Gurney precipitated a financial crisis, the threat of such a line receded. With the bank rate standing at ten per cent, new companies were unable to raise their authorised capital, and in these unhappy circumstances the Northampton & Banbury Junction promoters were unable to proceed with their expensive extension schemes. The idea of an extension from Banbury to Ross-on-Wye was not, however, abandoned, and in February 1871 the Northampton & Banbury Junction company proposed another £1,000,000 extension scheme.

At a time when the Midland and North Western companies were showing increasing interest in the neighbouring East & West Junction Railway, the Great Western viewed these developments with a certain unease, fearing, perhaps, that the Midland or L & NWR were still eager to launch some fresh offensive against GWR territory.

Meanwhile, the old tramway was stubbornly refusing to lie down and die. It continued to provide useful transport facilities for the small town of Shipston-on-Stour, and there was still some residual traffic on the 'main line' to Stratford. Operation remained informal, with local carriers providing services in the time-honoured way. Amusingly, all southbound journeys took place in the mornings, leaving the afternoons free for the northbound journeys! Various spurs and short sidings had been provided en route to facilitate overtaking, loading and unloading, and in the event of a conflicting movement these spurs would also have allowed up and down services to pass each other, most of the original passing places having by this time been removed.

Having wanted to close the tramway in the early 1860s, the Great Western later adopted a more sympathetic attitude, and by the 1870s, the Moreton to Shipston-on-Stour section seemed fairly secure. H. Weaver, who supervised the line from 1881 onwards, recalled that the Great Western 'had for some years prior to 1881, made considerable concessions to the Shipston traders by arranging through goods rates with that town, so that it was placed in the same position as any ordinary goods depot'. Writing in *The Great Western Magazine* in 1919, he remembered that 'through booked traffic was hauled over the tramway by the horses of the GWR local agents, either in through trucks or in private trucks provided by the local agents. Full truck loads of other traffic . . . which was not invoiced through to Shipston-on-Stour, was also conveyed over the tramway, the trucks being hauled by the horses of the individual traders who had to bring back the empty wagons to the railway, and pay small tonnage tolls for the use of the tramway'. Significantly, this reliable eyewitness made no mention of traffic working through from Moreton to Stratford-upon-Avon, though there must have been at least some activity on the northern part of the line in 1873, otherwise the East & West Junction Railway would not have built an expensive overbridge at Clifford Siding.

THE REVIVAL

In the 1880s, the GWR finally decided to bring the Moreton to Shipston section up to main line standards, placing the small town of Shipston-on-Stour on the Great Western network, and at the same time frustrating any further extensions of the East & West Junction or Northampton & Banbury Junction railways (or their main line allies).

It was necessary, before commencing work, for the Great Western to obtain Parliamentary consent, and on 3rd March 1882 *The Stratford-upon-Avon Herald* informed its readers that the 'Stratford & Moreton Railway Bill' was before Parliament, and had complied with standing orders. The 1882 Bill itself was a 'General Powers Bill' which, if successful, would confer various additional powers on the GWR. There

was, however, no reason to doubt that the Bill would have an easy passage through both Houses, and on 9th June 1882 *The Stratford-upon-Avon Herald* printed a further progress report, under the heading 'Shipston & Moreton Railway':

'The inhabitants of this neighbourhood will no doubt be pleased to hear that this scheme has not been forgotten, as we notice from *The Times* of Tuesday that the Great Western Bill (No 1), which includes the above, passed its third reading in the House of Lords, the only other stage remaining to go through being to get the Royal Assent.'

A week later, the paper caused something of a panic when it erroneously reported that the Great Western Railway (No 1) Bill had been 'thrown out after passing the third reading in the House of Lords'. Happily, the record was put straight on Friday 21st July, when the *Herald* published the following explanation:

'We are pleased to state that the Shipston and Moreton Railway Bill was not thrown out of Parliament, as stated in our last week's report, but that the obstruction to the measure was only temporary. It has now been overcome, and the 'Bill has been reinstated to a legal position. It seems that the Bill, having in some particulars failed to comply with the standing orders, was referred by the Examiner of Private Bills to the Select Committee on Standing Orders for their consideration and decision whether or not the standing orders might be dispensed with, and on Friday last the matter came before that committee, and after considering it in private the Chairman stated that the committee had decided to suspend the standing orders, to allow the Bill to proceed.'

The complex Parliamentary process was completed on Thursday, 10th August 1882, when the Great Western Railway (No 1) Bill received the Royal Assent.

The resulting Act of Parliament (45 & 46 Vic. Cap. 214) enabled the Great Western Railway to improve the circuitous Stratford & Moreton route by building a south-to-east curve at Darlingscott. This new line was defined in the Act as:

'A Railway . . . 2 furlongs 7.70 chains in length to be wholly situate in the township of Darlingscott in the parish of Tredington in the County of Worcestershire, commencing by a junction with the Stratford & Moreton Railway . . . and terminating by a junction with the Shipston-on-Stour branch of that Railway.'

Another provision in the 1882 Act allowed the Great Western to levy 'tolls and charges for goods and minerals . . . and for passengers', and it was stated that the tolls and charges for goods were to be 'as prescribed by the Stratford & Moreton Railway Act 1 & 2 George IV Cap 63', while passenger rates were to be as 'prescribed by the Oxford Worcester & Wolverhampton Act 1845'.

The people of Shipston-on-Stour were confident that, having obtained Parliamentary consent, the Great Western would soon start work on their branch, but before the modernisation process could begin, it was discovered that the 1833 Act for the construction of the Shipston branch *forbade the use of steam locomotives*. If a 'locomotive or other engine to be worked by the power of steam, or any other power than that of horses or other cattle' was to be used on the branch, the company would have to carry the line 'over or under any turnpike road by means of a bridge or tunnel'. As the Great Western intended to use the tramway in more or less its original form, a further Act was necessary, and until such an Act was obtained, the GWR would be unable to introduce steam traction on the Shipston-on-Stour branch.

The inhabitants of the little town were disappointed at the Great Western's failure to secure the necessary powers, and it is, in retrospect, astounding that the company's legal department should have failed to realise the full implications of the 1833 Act. Cynics may have wondered if the company was serious in its attempts to modernise the branch, but these lingering doubts were dispelled some two years later when (after considerable vacillation) the GW finally secured the requisite powers.

A FURTHER ACT OF PARLIAMENT

The Great Western (No 1) Act of 1884 (47 & 48 Vic. cap. 235) was, like its 1882 predecessor, a complex piece of legislation conferring a variety of different powers. On this occasion, however, a substantial section of the Act dealt with matters relating to the Stratford & Moreton Railway, and one must conclude that, having been made to look rather foolish in 1882, the company's lawyers had left nothing to chance. The problem vis-à-vis locomotives was covered in great detail, and an important section of the 1884 Act allowed the GWR to:

'. . . carry and convey passengers and goods, minerals and other traffic on their Stratford & Moreton Tramway . . . they may from time to time use on such parts of the said Tramway as lies between Moreton-in-Marsh and Shipston-on-Stour or any part or parts thereof, locomotives engines or other mechanical power, and carriages and wagons to be drawn or propelled thereby.'

The Act also permitted the company to:

'demand and take for and in respect of their Stratford & Moreton Tramway between Shipston-on-Stour and Moreton including the portion thereof authorised by the Great Western Railway (No 1) Act of 1882, for the use of the Tramway and of carriages and waggons or trucks and for locomotive power and for the conveyance on such Tramway of passengers, animals and goods, the same tolls, rates, fares and charges as the Company are authorised to demand and take for and in respect of their Oxford Worcester and Wolverhampton Railway under the Oxford Worcester and Wolverhampton Railway Act 1845.'

Significantly, the 1884 Act stipulated that any locomotives used on the Shipston-on-Stour line should, if practicable, 'consume their own smoke' and not exceed the speed of 20 miles per hour. Clearly, the new branch line was to be operated very much as a tramway or light railway, and although the Light Railways Act of 1896 had not yet been passed, certain provisions in the Great Western (No 1) Act of 1884 were similar to the provisions in the Tramways Act 1870, and the Regulation of Railways Act 1868. The relevant section of the 1884 Act may be worth quoting in detail; it imposed the following restrictions 'with respect to the use of locomotives or other mechanical power' on the Stratford & Moreton Tramway:

'Every engine used on the Tramway shall, if it use coal or other similar fuel emitting smoke, be constructed on the principle of consuming . . . as far as practicable its own smoke, and if any engine be not so constructed, the Company or party using such an engine shall forfeit Five pounds for every day which such engine shall be used on the Tramway.

'The speed at which engines or carriages may be driven or propelled along the Tramway shall not exceed the rate of Twenty miles per hour.

'The speed at which engines and carriages may pass over any level crossing shall not exceed the rate of Four miles per hour.

'The Board of Trade may on complaint made by any person from time to time inspect any engine used on the said portion of Tramway and the machinery therein and may whenever they think fit prohibit the use on the Tramway of any such engine which in their opinion may not be safe for use on the Tramway.'

Other relevant provisions of the 1884 Act dealt with the problem that had arisen in connection with level crossings and the Great Western's existing obligations under the 1833 Act; these obligations were ended by the following clause:

'Notwithstanding anything in the Act or Acts of Parliament or in any bye-laws or regulations to the contrary . . . the Company shall not be required to construct bridges over or tunnels under the level crossings or any of them on the aforesaid portion of the Stratford & Moreton Tramway, or maintain lodges or . . . employ any person or persons to open and shut gates at the level crossings or any of them on the aforesaid portion of such Tramway, but before opening the said Tramway for the conveyance of passengers thereon drawn or propelled by locomotive engines or other mechanical power, the Company shall make such bye-laws, rules and regulations with reference to the passage of traffic over the said level crossings as shall be approved by the Board of Trade.'

There was, perhaps, an ulterior motive behind the Great Western's apparent desire to retain the Shipston branch in being as a tramway. If the line was upgraded to main line standards it was possible that the Midland or some other expansionist company might seek running powers as part of some renewed attack on the GWR. Parliament would however be unlikely to grant such powers over a tramway, and thus the Great Western, in rebuilding the Shipston branch, was taking steps to block any Midland moves in that direction.

Having obtained the relevant powers, the Great Western started relaying its tramway with bullhead rail and cross sleepers. The tunnel at Campden Road was removed, and the new south-to-east curve was installed to the south of Ilmington. Leaving the old line at a point some 6 miles 34 chains from Moreton, this new curve turned sharply through 90 degrees and rejoined the Shipston branch near the hamlet of Darlingscott, allowing trains to run direct from Moreton to Shipston without reversing at Ilmington Junction. It is interesting to note that at least one small tank locomotive was used on the line during the course of these substantial alterations, the first recorded appearance of a steam locomotive at Shipston since Mr Sherriff's inspection trip in 1857.

RE-BUILDING THE BRANCH

Construction work proceeded in a curiously slow, perhaps even half-hearted manner, indicating that the Great

Tunnel Bridge shortly after its completion, probably around 1887. The deep cuttings visible in this photograph replaced the original tramway tunnel, but caused much trouble during the wet spring months of 1889 when the newly-formed earthworks showed a tendency to slip.
Shipston-on-Stour & District Local History Society

Western authorities viewed the Shipston scheme as a low priority project. Preliminary work commenced as early as March 1882, when *The Stratford-upon-Avon Herald* reported that orders had been given to have the tramway wharf at Shipston measured 'with a view to a station being erected there'. Thereafter the scheme remained in abeyance while the Great Western obtained its 1884 Act, but on 18th June 1886 the *Herald* was able to tell its readers that work was about to begin:

'At last we can authentically say that the much-talked-of railway to Shipston is close at hand, for the Great Western Railway Co. have now completed their agreements for the purchase of lands required by them. During the past few months the authorities have been very busy at Reading preparing sleepers, etc., for the line, and last week several thousands of metals, sleepers, etc., were brought to Moreton in readiness for the immediate construction of the line. It is a fact, we believe, that some parts of the line are now actually being laid down in readiness to take the place of the old metals. It is believed here that the line will be nearly completed by the end of the Autumn.'

Three months later *The Stratford-upon-Avon Herald* noted that the GWR was 'pushing forward' towards Shipston, and more than a mile of permanent way had already been laid at the Moreton end of the line; indeed, a locomotive was busily employed 'bringing the materials along the route'. Problems were soon encountered north of Stretton-on-Fosse, where the task of opening-out Campden Road Tunnel proved to

be more difficult than expected, but on 4th November 1887 the *Herald* printed the following progress report:

'The work on the old tramway is rapidly proceeding. The rails are laid as far as Darlingscott, and if the men are kept on, the work will soon be completed. The new bridge across the Campden Road, which has been in the course of erection for several months, is now nearly finished. There is some talk of widening Water Lane, Shipston, to make a better road to the station, and it is said that Mr George Bishop has offered land for this purpose, but the matter must come before the Highway Board.'

In the event, work did not proceed quite as 'rapidly' as the reporter had suggested, and twelve months later the line was still far from complete. People began to wonder if the GWR intended to abandon the scheme, and by 25th January 1889 a note of sarcasm was creeping into the *Herald*'s progress report:

'The railway is steadily progressing, and is nearly finished. A gang is at present putting up a tank for feeding the engine and fixing pumps, etc. As regards the opening the company are, as usual, taking things very quietly, and some day, when they have had plenty of time to think about it we may hear of it being opened.'

The pace of construction was, in truth, ridiculously slow, and it may be significant that the Great Western's interest in the project fluctuated in accordance with events on the nearby East & West Junction line. Thus in 1886, when the E & W

Jcn appeared to be undergoing a revival, the GWR started work on the Shipston branch. Great Western interest then appeared to wane, but in 1887, by which time the L & NWR (as well as the Midland) was tinkering with the East & West Junction and its allies, work was again well underway between Moreton and Shipston.

At the beginning of 1889, the GWR directors were, after seven years, able to tell their shareholders that 'the conversion of the Stratford & Moreton Tramway, between Moreton-in-the-Marsh and Shipston-on-Stour' was complete, and the 'steam tramway' was soon to be inspected by the Board of Trade, after which it could be opened to the public.

The forces of nature then intervened, and further work was impeded by a period of unusually wet spring weather which caused some of the newly-formed earthworks to collapse. On 8th May 1889 *The Oxfordshire Weekly News* noted that, after this unexpected setback, the Great Western was 'making rapid progress on the line'. Over forty navvies were at work repairing the various slips and placing ballast where it was required. The worst slips, claimed the paper, 'occurred at the Stretton Tunnel' where the deep cuttings were composed of soil that would 'take a long time to get firm'. Signals had been placed warning drivers to slacken speed to 'a pace of five miles an hour round the curves', and

An unidentified Great Western 0–6–0 saddle tank (probably a '645' class) beneath Tunnel Bridge, with its crew and what appear to be GWR engineering staff and contractor's officials. This picture was probably taken during the 1889 landslip.   *Cty. A. Boyce*

Moreton-in-Marsh c.1890, with the Shipston-on-Stour branch train visible in the background. Most of the station staff had gathered for the photographer, including the shunting horse. The locomotive appears to have been an 850 class 0—6—0ST.
Collection Mr. Kean

the general public were said to be waiting to hear when the line would be 'permanently opened for general traffic'.

RE-OPENING TO SHIPSTON-ON-STOUR

Happily, the slips at Campden Road proved to be the final obstacle, and on Saturday, 22nd June 1889 *The Oxford Chronicle* informed local people that the Shipston-on-Stour branch was, at long last, nearly finished:

'This line is now near completion, the double gates having been put up on all the level crossings, and the line is expected to be open for passenger traffic on July 1st.'

Having passed its Board of Trade inspection, the GWR opened the branch to public traffic on Monday, 1st July 1889. Shipston people were not officially told of the impending re-opening until the preceeding Saturday, and in the absence of advance warning it was impossible to arrange any special festivities; most local traders agreed to close their shops and premises, but the Great Western refused to provide a special excursion to mark the Great Day.

Unwilling to be totally deprived of the chance to celebrate, large numbers of local people turned out to see the 'First Train', and despite the Great Western's own lack of enthusiasm, Opening Day developed a momentum of its own,

becoming more of a carnival than anyone had intended. Several local newspapers reported the event, *The Oxfordshire Weekly News* providing one of the best accounts:

'At 7.05 on Monday morning the first train started, amidst great excitement, for Moreton-in-Marsh station, and many visitors arrived to take a first trip on the newly-constructed line, many going only to Longdon Road station, and walking back to breakfast. As the train started out of the station the event was announced far and wide by the exploding of fog signals and loud cheers ... the opening of the line has come about very suddenly, and proved to be a great and agreeable surprise; several flags were hung out at windows in different parts of the town as a festive demonstration in connection with the event, and it is expected the opening of the new line will prove favourable to the town and trade of Shipston-on-Stour and a great convenience to the whole neighbourhood, and our local auctioneers have announced the commencement of the monthly auction sales. Altogether it is expected the railway will be a great help to Shipston in the future.'

EARLY YEARS

The Oxford Chronicle reporter returned to Shipston a few weeks later, and on 27th July the paper printed another paragraph on the line in operation:

'The branch . . . is now in full swing. The Directors of the Great Western Railway Company have conferred a great favour upon the inhabitants of Shipston and the neighbourhood by giving excellent service with eight trains daily to and from Moreton. The line is substantially laid, and the travelling is rather slow at present, but remarkably

---

SHIPSTON-ON-STOUR AND MORETON-IN-THE-MARSH LOCOMOTIVE TRAMWAY.

Single Line—Worked by Train Staff.   No Block Telegraph.   Colour of Staff, Varnished Beech; Shape, Round.
Only one Engine in Steam or two Engines coupled together, allowed on this Tramway at the same time.
All Trains are mixed Trains, and convey Passengers, Goods, and Mineral Traffic.

| Distances. | | DOWN TRAINS. WEEK DAYS ONLY. | 1 | 2 | 3 | 4 | 5 | 6 |
Miles.	Chains		M	S				
			A.M.	A.M.	P.M.	P.M.	P.M.	
	14	Moreton-in-the Marsh ....dep.	9 8	9 35	1 5	5 10	8 20	....
1	50	Todenham Road Crossing ...... pass	—	—	—	—	—	...
2	66	Lemington Lane ,, ,,	—	—	—	—	—	...
4	16	Todenham Lane ,, ,,	—	—	—	—	—	...
4	68	Stretton-on-Fosse (Golden Cross) dep.	CR	CR	CR	CR	—	...
6	54	Stretton Road Crossing .... pass	—	—	—	—	—	..
7	6	Longdon Rd. Stn. (for Ilmington) dep.	9 38	10 5	1 35	5 40	8 50	...
7	57	Darlingscot Green Crossing .... pass	—	—	—	—	—	...
7	74	Fosse Road Crossing ,,	—	—	—	—	—	...
		Darlingscot and Shipston Road Crossing .... ,,	—	—	—	—	—	...
8	75	Shipston-on-Stour ....arr.	9 53	10 20	1 50	5 55	9 5	...

| Distances. | | UP TRAINS. WEEK DAYS ONLY. | 1 | 2 | 3 | 4 | 5 | 6 |
Miles.	Chains							
			A.M.	A.M.	P.M.	P.M.		
1	1	Shipston-on-Stour .... dep.	7 5	11 35	3 30	7 15	....	...
1	18	Darlingscot and Shipston Road Crossing................. ,,	—	—	—	—	..	...
1	69	Fosse Road Crossing .... ,,	—	—	—	—	..	...
2	21	Darlingscot Green Crossing .... ,,	—	—	—	—	..	...
4	7	Longdon Rd.Stn. (for Ilmington) dep.	7 20	11 50	3 45	7 30	....	...
4	69	Stretton Road Crossing .... ,,	—	—	—	—	..	...
6	9	Stretton-on-Fosse (Golden Cross) dep.	CR	CR	CR	—	..	...
7	25	Todenham Lane Crossing ...... pass	—	—	—	—	..	...
8	61	Lemington ,, ,, ... ,,	—	—	—	—	..	...
8	75	Todenham Road ,, ,,	—	—	—	—	..	...
		Moreton-in-the-Marsh .... arr.	7 50	12 20	4 15	8 0	....	...

M   Runs at these times except on Shipston-on-Stour stock sale days.

S   Runs at these times on Shipston-on-Stour sale days—viz., on October 15th, November 20th, December 18th, 1889; January 22nd, February 19th, March 19th, April 15th, May 21st, and June 23rd, 1890. On these days the 7.5 a.m. Train from Shipston-on-Stour will run light from Moreton-in-the-Marsh to Honeybourne to work a Special Passenger Train thence to Shipston-on-Stour, as under:—

									A.M.	
Moreton-in-the-Marsh	...	...	...	...	dep.	8 20	} Empty Train.
Honeybourne	...	...	...	...	...	arr.	8 45	
Honeybourne	...	...	...	...	...	dep.	9 5	
Campden	...	...	...	...	...	dep.	9 18	
Blockley	...	...	...	...			9 23	
Moreton-in-the-Marsh	...	...	...			arr.	9 30	Proceeding from

Moreton-in-the-Marsh to Shipston-on-Stour at 9.35 a.m. as shewn in column No. 2 Down.

The speed of Trains or Engines working over the Tramway must not exceed the rate of twenty miles per hour at any point and four miles per hour when passing over any Level Crossing.

The Speed must also be reduced to five miles an hour when passing round the sharp curves at Longdon Road, and at other places where Caution Boards have been fixed to warn Drivers.

See Special Instructions dated June 29th 1889, for WORKING THIS TRAMWAY.

The maximum loads over this Tramway in either direction are 10 Ten-ton Goods or Mineral Wagons, in addition to the Passenger Vehicles.

The gradients on this Tramway from Moreton-in-the-Marsh to Shipston-on-Stour are as shewn below :—

Between the 92 and 94 mile posts ...	...	1 in 68 Down.
,, 95 ,, 96¼ ,, ...	...	1 ,, 116 Up.
,, 96¼ ,, 97 ,, ...	...	1 ,, 76 Down.
,, 98 ,, 99 ,, ...	...	1 ,, 54 Down.
,, 100 ,, Shipston-on-Stour Station	...	1 ,, 79 Down.

As the gradients are heavy, the following instructions must be observed :—

All Trains descending the incline into Shipston-on-Stour Station must do so at a speed not exceeding five miles per hour.

The General Instructions for working these Inclines, contained in the Circular of the Superintendent of the Line, dated Sept., 1887, must be strictly observed.

NO. 3.

63

Service timetable for October 1889.

A branch train at Shipston, headed by the customary 850 class 0–6–0 saddle tank, at rest alongside the station building, c.1901. The horse-drawn cab on the platform was owned by Albert Paintin & Co. who were, according to Kelly's Directory of 1904, cab proprietors and coal merchants, and corn and flour dealers of New Street, Shipston. The cab conveyed passengers and parcels between the station and the George Hotel in Sheep Street. The George Hotel was the parcels receiving office of the GWR, F. S. Parsons acting as the company agent. At this time Mr. A. H. Smith was station master, presiding over six other members of staff under his supervision. *Railway Magazine*

easy. The coaches are comfortably fitted with every accommodation that is necessary for the convenience of the public. This quaint old town has been half a century behind the times, but it will now have communication with the outer world, and the steam line has already improved trade, property is increasing in value, and new buildings are under construction.'

When first opened, the line was subject to severe speed restrictions, but these were lifted as soon as the earthworks had settled down. However, as a light railway the line still carried an overall speed limit of twenty miles an hour, with numerous other restrictions on curves and level crossings.

The timetable at the time of opening, and indeed for many years thereafter, provided just four mixed trains each way daily. In October 1889, for example, trains left Shipston for Moreton at 7.05am, 11.35am, 3.30pm, and 7.15pm, while in the reverse direction the balancing down workings departed from Moreton-in-Marsh at 9.08am, 1.05pm, 5.10pm, and 8.20pm respectively. Journey time, for the 8 mile 75 chain journey, was 45 minutes. On 'sale days' at Shipston, the early morning up train reversed at Moreton and ran light to Honeybourne, returning from there as a special through train at 9.05am, and calling en route at Campden and Blockley.

Stations were provided at Shipston-on-Stour, Longdon Road and Stretton-on-Fosse, the latter being opened a few months later than the others. Standardised GW style wooden buildings were provided at all three stations, though, in view of the limited traffic expected, these structures offered only basic accommodation. Shipston, the largest station, boasted a miniature platform canopy.

Stretton-on-Fosse and Longdon Road station buildings measured approximately 30ft x 14½ft at ground level, whereas Shipston-on-Stour's building measured about 46ft x 14½ft overall. These three buildings were about 12ft high from ground sill to gutter level, and each contained the usual waiting rooms and offices. The toilets at Longdon Road were

Railway Magazine

accommodated within the main structure, but at Stretton-on-Fosse and Shipston-on-Stour they were situated in extensions which projected from the main buildings.

In common with many other station buildings erected by the GWR in the late Victorian period, Shipston, Stretton-on-Fosse and Longdon Road stations had no rear entrances, and travellers wishing to purchase tickets had, perforce, to enter from the platforms.

A single-road locomotive shed was provided at Shipston-on-Stour, and surprisingly, in view of the primitive station building, this shed was solidly constructed of red brick. Other features of the rebuilt branch included several brick-built cottages for the level crossing gate keepers, and a relatively large, corrugated iron goods shed at Shipston-on-Stour. There were nine public level crossings, several over or underbridges, and a bridge across the Knee Brook near Stretton-on-Fosse.

TRAINS AND TRAFFIC

The original train service persisted, with only minor variations, throughout the first decades. In 1907 the first up working left Shipston at 6.35am, and having pursued its leisurely way through the Edwardian countryside, it reached Moreton-in-Marsh at 7.20am. After a lengthy pause, the train returned to Shipston at 9.20am. The next up service departed from Shipston at 11.05am, reaching the junction by 11.50am and returning at 1.15pm. There was a further return working at 3.25pm, arriving back at Shipston by 5.50pm. Finally, the last up train of the day left Shipston at 6.45pm and returned from Moreton-in-Marsh at 8.15pm. One or two of the services were extended along the main line to Honeybourne on market days, but this practice never became general; there was no Sunday service and no separate freight services, 'We didn't have goods only trains – only mixed or passenger' remembered Shipston fireman George Lysons.

A connection to the horse-worked northern section of the tramway was retained via Longdon Road goods yard, which thus became an interchange point between the two halves of the tramway. It is most unlikely that such traffic

---

SHIPSTON-ON-STOUR AND MORETON-IN-MARSH LOCOMOTIVE TRAMWAY.

Single Line—Worked by Train Staff.   No Block Telegraph.   Colour of Staff, Varnished Beech; Shape, Round.   Only one Engine in Steam or two Engines coupled together, allowed on this Tramway at the same time.

Distances.		DOWN TRAINS. WEEK DAYS ONLY.		1 B Mixed. S.T. 31	2 B Passenger.	3	4 B Mixed.	5 B Passenger.	6	7
Miles.	Chns.			A.M.	P.M.		P.M.	P.M		
		Moreton-in-Marsh	dep.	9 20	1 15	....	5 5	8 15	....	....
	14	Todenham Road Crossing	pass.	—	—	..	—	—	..	..
	40	Stop Board Top of Incline	dep.	—	—	....	—	—	..	....
1	50	Lemington Lane	pass.	—	—	..	—	—	..	...
2	66	Todenham Lane	,,	—	—	..	—	—	..	...
4	12	Stretton-on-Fosse	dep.	9 40	1 35	..	5 25	8 35	..	..
4	68	Stretton Road Crossing..	pass.	—	—	....	—	—	..	..
6	34	Stop Board Top of Incline	,,	—	—	....	—	—	..	..
6	54	Longdon Road (for Ilmington)	dep.	9 50	1 45	....	5 35	8 45	....	....
7	6	Darlingscot Green Crossing	pass.	—	—	..	—	—	..	..
7	57	Fosse Road Crossing	,,	—	—	....	—	—	..	..
7	74	Darlingscot and Shipston Road Crossing	,,	—	—	....	—	—	..	..
8	75	Shipston-on-Stour	arr.	10 5	2 0	....	5 50	9 0	....	....

UP TRAINS. WEEK DAYS ONLY.		1 B Passenger.	2 B Mixed.	3	4 B Mixed.	5 B Passenger.	6	7
		A.M.	A.M.		P.M.	P.M		
Shipston-on-Stour	dep.	6 35	11 5	....	3 25	6 45	....	....
Darlingscot and Shipston Road Crossing	pass.	—	—	..	—	—	..	..
Fosse Road Crossing	,,	—	—	....	—	—	..	..
Darlingscot Green Crossing	,,	—	—	....	—	—	..	..
Longdon Road (for Ilmington)	dep.	6 50	11 20	....	3 40	7 0	....	....
Stop Board Top of Incline	,,	—	—	..	—	—	..	..
Stretton Road Crossing..	pass.	—	—	....	—	—	..	..
Stretton-on-Fosse	dep.	7 0	11 30	..	3 50	7 10	..	..
Todenham Lane Crossing	pass.	—	—	..	—	—	..	..
Lemington ,, ,, ...	,,	—	—	....	—	—	..	..
Stop Board Top of Incline	,,	—	—	....	—	—	....	....
Todenham Road ,, ...	,,	—	—	..	—	—	..	..
Moreton-in-Marsh	arr.	7 20	11 50	....	4 10	7 30	....	....

Speed Restrictions—Shipston-on-Stour Line.

With reference to page 37 of Appendix to No. 14 Service Book, the Speed Restrictions on this Branch are as shown below :—

The Speed of Trains or Engines working over the Tramway must not exceed the rate of 20 miles per hour at any point, and 4 miles per hour when passing over any of the Nine Level Crossings.

The Speed must also be reduced to 5 miles an hour when passing the points shown below :—

	Miles.	Chains.		Miles.	Chains.
Board from	92	75	to	93	1
,, ,,	97	40	,,	97	48
,, ,,	97	64	,,	97	73

Stop Dead Boards are fixed at 92 miles 29½ chains and 98 miles 6¼ chains.

Service timetable for January 1907.

This picture from a cracked glass negative reveals many interesting details of Stretton-on-Fosse station c.1907. The station master here around 1905 was Charles Cotton, though by 1916 he had been replaced by Mr. J. T. Hills. An 1896 reference suggests that the station was originally supervised by a 'booking constable'. The porter c.1916 was E. H. Shadbolt.   *The Shakespeare Birthplace Trust*

Another view of this tiny station, facing towards Moreton-in-Marsh in the Edwardian era. The station nameboard was probably white enamel with blue lettering.   *Lens of Sutton*

The Golden Cross Inn in the Edwardian period, showing the blue brick weigh-house built in 1906.   *The Shakespeare Birthplace Trust*

continued through to Stratford-upon-Avon, but there may have been occasional consignments from intermediate points on the tramway such as Newbold Lime Works or Clifford Siding.

In its early years as a 'locomotive tramway' (as it was called in GWR working timetables) the Shipston-on-Stour branch was worked by small 0-6-0 saddle tanks, usually members of the '850' class. These engines were provided by Worcester shed and sub-shedded at Shipston.

According to George Lysons, who was sent to Shipston as a young fireman in 1908, 'they used to replace the engine about every twelve months. They used to do them up and put them in good nick, then they'd last the year. The sharp curves used to wear the tyres and one thing and another. Then they'd need some fitters work after a week or two and a fitter and his mate would come down from Worcester on a Friday night and go back the next day. A boiler smith used to come every month to examine the boiler. In those days we used to call those shunting engines 'Jackos' – one I remember was 1216.'

There were four loco men based at Shipston to cover the branch services, one driver, a passenger fireman who drove one trip and two firemen. They worked in shifts from 3.05am to 1.05pm and from 1.05pm to 11.05pm, the passenger fireman always working the late shift. The driver and the passenger fireman washed out the boiler of the branch engine on a Sunday when it was out of steam and not required. One turned the water on and off while the other went round the washout plugs. Apart from emergencies, this

An earlier platform view facing Shipston and featuring the ivy-clad Golden Cross Inn. This summertime period picture was probably taken c.1907.   *D. Burge, Shipston Historical Society*

was the only time the water supply at Shipston was used, water normally being taken at Moreton where the supply was more suitable. The well supplying the pillar tank at Shipston was unreliable and ran dry in the summer of 1911. For occasions like this, a spare tender was kept at Shipston full of water. 'I don't think we used it above twice. We had to fetch water from Moreton and let it down the well then pump it up into the tank.' The pump was powered by steam from the branch engine by means of a flexible pipe coupled in place of one of the whistles.

The small saddle tanks demanded careful attention. 'It was a work of art to fire them. If you put a shovel wrong you were done for and they wouldn't carry much water'. In comparison George Lysons recalled how things improved later: 'In between the wars everything was as near perfect as possible – you got better engines. They were modern engines in good nick'. George also recalled how the branch engine was kept pretty busy during the day. 'When we got to Moreton you'd be surprised at the amount of shunting that had to be done, then we came back to Shipston and shunted the yard there. My mate (George's driver) lived in the terrace just past the station . . . when it was time to do the shunting he used to go off for a cup of tea and leave me on my own to do the work'.

Regular Shipston drivers, in the years before World War One, included William Bennett and G. Pursey, while the usual guard was George Salisbury of Shipston-on-Stour.

The branch functioned successfully throughout the 1890s and early 1900s when, in an age without road competition, its circuitous route and hopelessly slow trains continued to attract modest levels of passenger traffic. In 1898, for example, Shipston-on-Stour booked 6,131 passengers and handled 15,682 tons of freight. These annual totals compared favourably with those from the smaller OW & WR main line stations such as Adlestrop and Ascott-under-Wychwood, which handled on average about 5,000 passengers and 3,000 tons of freight per annum during the period under review. On the other hand, other OW & WR stations were much busier than Shipston, particularly in terms of passenger traffic. In 1903, for instance, Campden booked 12,833

passenger tickets, which was twice as many as Shipton-on-Stour at the turn of the century.

From the Great Western's point of view, the Shipston-on-Stour branch must have been something of a disappointment, and even in its heyday, this very rural line would have been no more than marginally profitable. However, the railway was a valuable public amenity, contributing countless unseen local benefits, and it is clear that without the railway Shipston would have been in a condition bordering on economic stagnation.

It is possible to see how the branch contributed to Shipston's economy by studying the station's 1898 and 1899 traffic returns which have fortuitously survived. The original documents show all types of goods and passenger traffic, both inwards and outwards, and also show all receipts and expenses for the years concerned. Although, in their original form, they are difficult to read, it is possible to extract much interesting detail. For convenience this information is summarised in *Table 3*.

The basic types of 'passenger' traffic (people, parcels and domestic animals) are self-explanatory, but the curious groups of goods traffic may require explanation: briefly, 'Coal & Coke Charged' referred to coal traffic paid for at the start of its journey. The small amount of coal sent *from* Shipston would have been despatched by local coal merchants to other coal depots in the vicinity; 'Other Minerals' included stone and building materials, while 'Carted Traffic' referred to all kinds of general merchandise including timber from Mayos 'who used to make a lot of Windsor chair seats and send them to High Wycombe'; finally, 'Not Carted Traffic' consisted of

TABLE 3: TRAFFIC HANDLED AT SHIPSTON-ON-STOUR IN 1898 & 1899				
TYPES OF TRAFFIC	INWARDS		OUTWARDS	
	1898	1899	1898	1899
PASSENGER TICKETS	-	-	6,328	6,131
PARCELS	5,733	6,481	2,843	3,367
HORSES, CARRIAGES, DOGS & MISCELLANEOUS TRAFFIC	30	268	1,922	1,854
COAL & COKE CHARGED	128 tons	156 tons	21 tons	123 tons
COAL & COKE NOT CHARGED	5,158 tons	5,295 tons	-	-
OTHER MINERAL (stone, slates, etc.)	1,420 tons	4,386 tons	12 tons	65 tons
CARTED TRAFFIC (paper, sugar, nails, general supplies, etc.)	1,302 tons	1,281 tons	334 tons	335 tons
NOT CARTED TRAFFIC (corn, hay, straw, potatoes)	2,340 tons	2,624 tons	1,484 tons	1,417 tons
LIVE STOCK	20 wagons	14 wagons	39 wagons	48 wagons

TOTAL GOODS TONNAGE	12,199 tons (1898)	15,682 (1899)
RECEIPTS (GOODS)	£4,398 (1898)	£5,229 (1899)
RECEIPTS (PASSENGER)	£1,296 (1898)	£1,381 (1899)
TOTAL RECEIPTS	£5,694 (1898)	£6,610 (1899)

A view northwards along the horse-worked northern section of the S & M tramway near Clifford Chambers c.1904.

Warwick County Record Office

bulk loads such as hay or grain which would have been collected or delivered to the station by farmers' or traders' vehicles (ie not carted by the GWR or its local agents).

The traffic returns did not indicate what forms of 'Not Carted Traffic' were handled at Shipston, but in an agricultural area it is likely that the main kinds of outwards traffic would have been the corn and hay. Hay was, in fact, an important export in any rural area, and at a time when the United Kingdom had over 3,250,000 horses, the importance of this commodity will be obvious. Livestock traffic was not, perhaps, as extensive as one might expect, and in 1898 only 39 cattle wagons were despatched, suggesting that local farms were primarily arable.

Excursions were occasionally advertised from Shipston to London or other destinations, but in practice these were excursion *tickets* rather than special trains. The first such excursion ran on Monday, 16th September 1889, when eighty people took advantage of a special fare offer to London. The excursionists, many of whom were employees of the Candle Well Brewery on a works outing, left Shipston on the 7.00am up train and changed into an up special Shrewsbury to Paddington excursion at Moreton-in-Marsh. The fare on this occasion was just five shillings and the excursionists returned home in the early hours of Tuesday morning, necessitating a special connecting service from Moreton to Shipston.

Similar excursion fares were offered in subsequent years, the usual price being five shillings return. Country people could not, in general, afford to take holidays and there were no mass summer migrations from Shipston to the seaside. Day trips were, on the other hand, looked forward to, favoured destinations being Weston-super-Mare or Portsmouth, the most convenient seaside venues for Shipston people.

When returning excursionists missed the evening down train from Moreton-in-Marsh, the usual procedure was for the ordinary branch train to run empty from Shipston to Moreton in order to provide a connection at the junction.

Like most rural branch lines, the Shipston-on-Stour branch served the community in perfect safety for many years, but minor accidents sometimes took place, and these were often reported by local papers. On 17th October 1890, for instance, *The Stratford-upon-Avon Herald* recounted a mishap that had recently taken place at Shipston:

'ACCIDENT – On Monday last an accident to the engine driver, G. Pursey, occurred at the station. He was on an iron ladder at the tank, and in some way lost his balance and fell backwards. Luckily, at the time of falling he made a spring and alighted on his feet. He was very much shaken, and his shoulder was injured, incapacitating him from work. We understand that he is recovering.'

Although contemporary readers may have felt that this incident was hardly a world-shattering event, the *Herald* report is of some interest in that it refers by name to the branch's first regular engine driver.

The old tramway terminus and bridge at Stratford-upon-Avon in 1892. Before the extensive basin in the foreground had been turned into a pleasure garden, the tramway extended past the site of the bandstand and alongside the path in the centre of the picture. The tramway bridge can be seen in the right background, together with the famous Clopton Bridge, which had been built by Sir Hugh Clopton in the reign of Henry VII. This photograph was taken from the original Shakespeare Memorial Theatre, built in 1879 and largely destroyed by fire in 1926.

F. Frith

An incident of another kind was referred to by *The Oxfordshire Weekly News* on 9th January 1895. On this occasion the first up train of the day had failed to depart from Shipston at the usual time, and the paper, which was clearly running short of *real* news, saw fit to describe this trivial incident in detail:

'SHIPSTON-ON-STOUR - The train that should have left the station at 7 o'clock in the morning did not start until about 8 o'clock, to the inconvenience of several passengers who wanted to catch the London train at Moreton-in-Marsh. It is said the engine could not get up steam, a rather unusual thing on a railway.'

EXTENSION TO STRATFORD?

The Shipston-on-Stour branch would have been ideally suited to railmotor operation, and in 1904, when such vehicles were at the height of their popularity, the Great Western considered introducing a steam railmotor service between Moreton, Shipston and possibly Stratford-upon-Avon. Railmotors were already in use on OW & WR line services and it would have been a logical step to extend these services onto the branch. With this thought in mind, the GWR commenced clearing undergrowth and other obstructions from the tramway between Longdon Road and Stratford-upon-Avon. In July 1904, a group of high-ranking Great Western engineers inspected the proposed railmotor route, while at the same time the company was conducting a certain amount of market research among potential travellers.

Under the terms of the Light Railways Act the Government was empowered to provide financial help for such a line, and with interest being shown by local authorities it seemed that the entire tramway might have been rebuilt. Local residents were very enthusiastic, and there is no doubt that a railmotor service between Shipston and Stratford would have been well supported by Shipston people, Stratford, rather than Moreton-in-Marsh, being the area's main trading centre. Few Shipston residents had cause to travel regularly to Moreton.

The Stratford-upon-Avon Herald reported that 'large bodies of men' were at work on 'the old tram line between Longdon Road station and Stratford-on-Avon', and on 22nd July 1904 the paper printed the following brief report:

'There has been much talk recently of re-opening the Shipston-on-Stour and Stratford Tramway as a light railway, and as it has recently been cleared and inspected by the GWR inspectors, it looks as if there might be some truth in the report. Anyway, it seems a great pity to let the line remain in its present condition.'

In physical terms the work of upgrading the existing tramway would have been accomplished relatively easily – the only problem being the means of entry to Stratford. One solution might have been a small terminus on the east bank of the River Avon, though the service could well have been extended across the Tramway Bridge and into Bancroft Gardens. Alternatively, the East & West Junction Railway could have provided a ready-made path into the Great Western station at Stratford.

Sadly, the railmotor scheme was never put into effect, and one assumes that the earlier Acts forbidding the use of locomotives had presented insurmountable difficulties. There were, in particular, problems associated with the roadside section of the tramway, and Robert Hudson, who probably knew more about the Stratford & Moreton Railway than any other Great Western official, was convinced that a complete conversion would be totally impracticable. Writing in the March 1889 *Great Western Magazine* he said that it was often asked, 'why not convert the tramway through to Stratford-on-Avon, seeing that it passes through a district where a railway would be very welcome?'. The answer, he suggested, was that:

'Between Shipston-on-Stour and Stratford-on-Avon the tramway takes a route which presents physical difficulties to conversion which did not exist at the Moreton end. For several miles it runs open to the public highway – passing sometimes, as in the village of Alderminster, within two or three feet of cottage doors – and therefore conversion would mean deviation, land purchase and entire reconstruction.'

PASSENGER COUNT — Week ending Saturday, 20th September 1913								
Passengers leaving Shipston							*Average passengers*	
							leaving	*arriving*
Shipston	Mon	Tue	Wed	Thu	Fri	Sat	*Shipston*	*Moreton*
6.35	5	1	—	2	1	—	1	1
11.35	10	4	7	4	7	16	8	11
3/25	5	14	10	2	6	10	8	7
7/0	6	2	3	2	1	4	3	3
Passengers arriving Shipston							*Average passengers*	
							leaving	*arriving*
							Moreton	*Shipston*
9.22	7	5	12	6	7	9	7	8
1/15	7	19	7	8	5	18	8	11
5/5	18	4	1	1	5	15	8	7
8/10	7	4	4	7	6	5	6	6

Photographs of trains on the branch before the withdrawal of passenger services are very rare, so this one taken at Shipston-on-Stour before the Great War is particularly welcome. The official coach working programme for summer 1911 gave the following details: 'Shipston to Moreton (4 trips each way). 8-wheel Brake Compo. A milk truck to work on 6.55 p.m. ex Shipston daily, sent to Paddington on 4.50 Wolverhampton from Moreton.' According to the 1922 coach working book, a 6-wheel brake compo was provided for the following services: Shipston–Moreton, 7.20 a.m. Moreton–Shipston, 8.15 a.m. Shipston–Moreton, 9.57 a.m. Moreton–Shipston, 11.50 a.m. Shipston–Moreton, 5.0 p.m. Moreton–Shipston, 6.15 p.m. Shipston–Moreton.

Packer Studio

CHAPTER FOUR

TWENTIETH CENTURY DEVELOPMENTS
(1914-1948)

THE heyday of the Shipston-on-Stour branch lasted for just twenty-five years, and in retrospect, the down turn in its fortunes came in 1914-18; as in so many other spheres of British life, the Great War was a catalyst, bringing in its wake a period of acute decline.

WORLD WAR ONE

On 4th August 1914 the German Army entered Belgium, and, in response to this brutal and unprovoked attack on a harmless, neutral country, the British Government declared war on the aggressors. The war did not, at first, produce any adverse effects on the Shipston-on-Stour branch. There was, for example, no immediate black-out, and the thought that civilised people such as Germans would eventually commence aerial bombing of civilian targets would, in 1914, have been unthinkable. However, the railway soon began to carry increasing numbers of soldiers, as young men from Shipston and the surrounding villages responded to their country's call to arms. Some apparently joined in Shipston, but many travelled further afield to Oxford, Worcester and other major centres.

In accordance with contemporary practice, men from Shipston were encouraged to join their local regiment, the idea being that 'Pals' units would produce better results in the ordeal to come. Later, when the war began to take its toll, it became clear that 'Pals' units were not such a good idea after all, and they usually resulted in large numbers of men from the same localities being slaughtered together, doing little for morale on the home front.

As the casualty lists grew longer, the meaning of total war became clear even in rural communities such as Shipston and Moreton, and in January 1917, in a climate of growing wartime austerity, train services were cut. From New Year's Day the only trains running on the branch were, in the down direction, the 9.30am and 5.00pm from Moreton-in-Marsh, and in the up direction the 10.10am and 6.10pm from Shipston-on-Stour.

The reduced service of the two trains each way enabled further cuts to be made, and in a search for further economies Shipston engine shed and Stretton-on-Fosse station were both closed for the duration. The withdrawal of passenger services from Stretton was unpopular with local travellers, but, in spite of an appeal to the GWR, the General Manager decided that the station should remain closed. It was reported that receipts in 1915 had only been £669, of which only £236 was attributable to passenger traffic. These cuts in services brought staff changes in their wake, and Mr Hills, the station master at Stretton-on-Fosse, was transferred to another district.

The revised pattern of train services meant that drivers and guards were no longer stationed at Shipston and, although most of those involved were willing to move elsewhere on the GWR system, George Salisbury, the regular Shipston branch guard, decided to retire. This was indeed a break with the past, for Mr Salisbury had worked on the Shipston-on-Stour line for no less than 28 years. In view of this long period of service to the community, *The Stratford-upon-Avon Herald* printed the following tribute:

> 'Travellers on the Shipston branch will hear with great regret of the retirement of the genial and obliging guard, Mr G. Salisbury, who, by his invariable kindness and courtesy, had been the personal friend of a generation of passengers. Mr Salisbury joined the staff of the GWR forty-eight years ago, and was stationed at Worcester until the Shipston branch was opened for passenger traffic in 1889, when he came to the town as a guard, and held the position until the recent changes in the working of the traffic rendered a guard at Shipston unnecessary, when he was offered another good position as guard at a distant place, but being so attached to the town where he had lived for so many years, he decided to retire and make room for a younger man, and the townspeople, by whom he is generally well liked and respected, wish him health and every enjoyment of his well-earned rest.'

In April 1917 there was a further small change in branch timetables when the morning up working was retimed to depart from Shipston at 11.30am instead of 10.10am. Of greater significance was the lifting of what was left of the disused tramway between Longdon Road and Stratford-upon-Avon, and this melancholy result of the wartime search for scrap metal was accomplished by 1918.

Meanwhile, the conflict in Europe was drawing to a close, and on 11th November 1918 the guns on the Western Front fell silent. The Great War had cost over 1,000,000 British dead, and few towns or villages in the British Isles had been spared. Shipston lost many men, and the long list of names on the town's war memorial records the names of those who gave their lives. Most would have made their last journeys to the Channel ports by train.

JULY 1918

Two trains in each direction over the branch. The engine came from Worcester and worked as follows:

5.25	Worcester	Moreton-in-Marsh	7.40	Goods
	Shunt, Moreton-in-Marsh			
9.25	Moreton-in-Marsh	Shipston-on-Stour	10.5	Mixed, ST 31
11.30	Shipston-on-Stour	Moreton-in-Marsh	12/10	Mixed
12/20	Moreton-in-Marsh	Kingham	12/35	Lt. Eng.
1/10	Kingham	Chipping Norton	1/28	Mixed
3/5	Chipping Norton	Kingham	3/15	Passenger
3/20	Kingham	Moreton-in-Marsh	3/30	Lt. Eng.
5/0	Moreton-in-Marsh	Shipston-on-Stour	5/40	Mixed
6/10	Shipston-on-Stour	Moreton-in-Marsh	6/50	Mixed
	Shunt, Moreton-in-Marsh			
10/0	Moreton-in-Marsh	Worcester	12.10	Goods

THE LINE IN OPERATION, 1914-1929

The rapid development of road motor transport in the years following World War One soon made inroads into the line's modest passenger business, and in 1920 there were only two trains each way, taking up to 45 minutes for their 8¾ mile journey between Moreton and Shipston-on-Stour. This meagre service was in effect merely a continuation of the 1917 emergency timetable, with departures from Moreton at 9.57am and 5.00pm, and return workings from Shipston at 11.50am and 6.20pm respectively. Both trains were mixed workings conveying passenger and goods vehicles – a typical formation being a solitary bogie coach, with perhaps two open wagons, a van, and the customary 'Toad' brake van.

Stretton-on-Fosse was reopened after the war, but the line's two intermediate stations were, by that time, treated as halts as far as the passengers were concerned, and although both remained staffed it is unclear if tickets were still issued.

By July 1922 the early morning passenger train had been restored, and in the next few years the line enjoyed a slightly improved service of three trains each way.

For a time, the revived 7.27am departure from Moreton ran as a passenger-only service, the freedom from intermediate shunting allowing it to reach Shipston in the record time of thirty-three minutes. This unexpected acceleration was, perhaps, too good to last, and within a year the timetable had been reorganised to provide three mixed trains each way, with down services from Moreton at 10.05am, 1.15pm and 5.00pm. In the up direction, trains left Shipston at 11.50am,

JULY 1922				
Engine working:				
4.35	Worcester	Moreton-in-Marsh	6.45	Goods
7.27	Moreton-in-Marsh	Shipston-on-Stour	8.0	Passenger
8.15	Shipston-on-Stour	Moreton-in-Marsh	8.50	Passenger
9.57	Moreton-in-Marsh	Shipston-on-Stour	10.42	Mixed, ST 31
11.50	Shipston-on-Stour	Moreton-in-Marsh	12/35	Mixed
1/15	Moreton-in-Marsh	Campden	2/15	Goods
3/0	Campden	Moreton-in-Marsh	3/17	Goods
	Shunt, Moreton-in-Marsh			
5/0	Moreton-in-Marsh	Shipston-on-Stour	5/45	Mixed
6/15	Shipston-on-Stour	Moreton-in-Marsh	7/0	Mixed
	Shunt, Moreton-in-Marsh			
10/0	Moreton-in-Marsh	Worcester	12.25	Goods
(but earlier if ready)				

SHIPSTON-ON-STOUR AND MORETON-IN-MARSH LOCOMOTIVE TRAMWAY.

Single Line—Worked by Train Staff. No Block Telegraph. Colour of Staff, Varnished Beech.
Shape, Round.

Only one Engine in Steam or two Engines coupled together, allowed on this Tramway at the same time.

Distances.		DOWN TRAINS.	Station No.	1 B	2	3 B	4	5	6
Miles.	Chns.	WEEK DAYS ONLY.		Mxd.		Mxd.			
				A.M.		P.M.			
—	—	Moreton-in-Marsh .. .. dep.	6012	10 5	..	5 5	....	...	...
—	12	Todenham Road Crossing .... pass.	—	—	..	—	....	...	...
—	38	Stop Board Top of Incline .... dep.	—	—	..	—	....	...	...
1	48	Lemington Lane .. .. pass.	—	—	..	—	....	...	...
2	54	Todenham Lane .. .. "	—	—	..	—	....	...	...
4	12	Stretton-on-Fosse .... dep.	6119	10 25	..	5 25	....	..	...
4	66	Stretton Road Crossing .. .... pass.	—	—	..	—	....	..	...
6	34	Stop Board Top of Incline .... "	—	—	..	—	....	..	...
6	54	Longdon Road (for Ilmington) .... dep.	6120	10 35	....	5 35	....	..	...
7	4	Darlingscot Green Crossing .. .... pass.	—	—	....	—	....	..	...
7	16	Fosse Road Crossing .... "	—	—	....	—	....	..	...
7	72	Darlingscot and Shipston Road Crossing "	—	—	....	—	....	..	...
8	75	Shipston-on-Stour .. .. arr.	6121	10 45	....	5 50	....	..	...

Distances.		UP TRAINS.		1 B	2	3 B	4	5
Miles.	Chns.	WEEK DAYS ONLY.		Mxd.		Mxd.		
				A.M.		P.M.		
1	3	Shipston-on-Stour .. .... dep.		11 40	..	6 15	..	....
1	19	Darlingscot and Shipston Road Crossing .. .... pass.		—	....	—	..	....
1	71	Fosse Road Crossing .... "		—	....	—	..	....
2	21	Darlingscot Green Crossing .... "		—	....	—	..	....
4	9	Longdon Road (for Ilmington) .... dep.		11 55	..	6 30	..	....
4	63	Stretton Road Crossing.. .... pass.		—	..	—	..	....
6	11	Stretton-on-Fosse .... dep		12 5	..	6 40	..	....
7	27	Todenham Lane Crossing .... pass.		—	..	—	..	....
8	63	Lemington " "		—	..	—	..	....
8	75	Todenham Road "		—	..	—	..	....
		Moreton-in-Marsh .. .. arr.		12 25	..	7 0	..	....

All wagons from Shipston-on-Stour for Longdon Road must be taken to Moreton-in-Marsh and be worked back by first available train.

When there is no room in the siding at Stretton-on-Fosse, the wagons must be taken through to Moreton-in-Marsh.

Wagons for the direction of Moreton-in-Marsh may be gravitated from the siding to the train provided only the tail of the train (goods vehicles and brake van) is left on the Main Line on the Shipston-on-Stour side of the points.

Great care must be exercised when gravitating the wagons from the siding to the train.

If it is necessary to perform any shunting before wagons are gravitated out of the sidings, the passenger coaches must be left on the train, and the work carried out by the light engine.

Service timetable for 1922.

Passengers waiting at Longdon Road to board a Saturday excursion for Weston-super-Mare. Seaside trips were a regular feature of branch operation, although it should be stressed that such excursions usually originated at Worcester or elsewhere, and excursionists were conveyed to Moreton by the usual branch train.

2.50pm and 6.15pm. The fastest time was now forty minutes (the 10.05am down working) but other services were still allowed forty-five minutes.

The Shipston-on-Stour branch was always operated in the simplest possible manner, with no block telegraph and few signals – though in later years the stations were linked by telephone. Safe working of the single line was ensured by a wooden train staff, only one train being allowed on the branch at any one time. The line was, in essence, a steam-worked 'basic railway' with few of the expensive trimmings usually found on traditional Victorian-style branch lines.

Signalling, on this rural route, was simple in the extreme with a solitary home signal positioned some 200 yards from the platform at Shipston-on-Stour. According to George Lysons, 'you pulled it off by a lever on the platform – anyone could use it. If you'd gone by, it didn't really matter because you knew you'd got the road'. There were only four other semaphore signals on the branch – these were the down starter, up home and up distant signals at Moreton-in-Marsh, and a down distant at Shipston-on-Stour.

Although the line's three stations were linked by telephone, this refinement did not, in general, extend to the isolated level crossings, and most of the crossing keepers were unable to communicate with each other or with neighbouring stations. Under these circumstances, the crossing gates were normally kept open for road traffic until trains were due, at which times the crossing keepers would emerge from their cottages to close the gates. Appendices to the working time-tables reveal that 'in order to prevent undue delay, foot passengers, horsemen, and light vehicular traffic' were allowed to pass over the crossings 'until such time' as it was necessary to shut the gates for the passage of a train. When trains were

late, drivers were instructed to whistle when approaching each crossing, and 'regulate the speed of the train so as to be able to stop dead before reaching the crossing if the gates are across the railway'. Crossing keepers were exhorted to 'keep a good look out for both trains and road vehicles, and work their gates in the best way consistent with safety to prevent delays'.

When special trains were run the station masters in charge of each crossing were responsible for ensuring that each crossing keeper was issued with a working notice with details of each additional working, and, as mentioned in the previous chapter, such specials often returned in the early hours of the morning. If the homeward-bound excursions were late, the unfortunate crossing keepers would be unable to go to bed and, moreover, there would be no way of knowing what had happened to the delayed trains, or what time they would appear out of the night with their whistles shrieking.

Similar problems of communication arose during prolonged engineering work on the single line. As a general rule, the engineering department was allowed absolute occupation of the branch at the cessation of daily train services, but if work was not completed before the start of the following day's timetable, gangers were instructed to 'advise the station master by telephone or otherwise' when the line was clear. For this purpose fixed telephones were installed in tiny sentry boxes at intervals along the branch. The ganger was provided with a 'Velocipede Inspection Car' in order that he

Ganger Charles Webb on his velocipede at Longdon Road c.1925. He was killed on his velocipede when the daily goods train, which left Moreton-in-Marsh at 1.35 p.m., caught up with him on the approach to Longdon Road. The accident, which took place on 3rd February 1930, is detailed in Appendix 3.

Longdon Road station, looking east towards Shipston-on-Stour on 20th July 1920. The standard GWR corrugated iron shed was provided for use as a goods lock-up shed in October 1902 at a cost of £30. The station nameboard with its raised lettering was a different style to the enamel one at Stretton-on-Fosse. *R. K. Cope*

Longdon Road station, looking west towards the level crossing c.1934. At that time, the station was staffed by a porter.
Lens of Sutton

could inspect his own length of track each day (Sundays excepted). These unusual vehicles resembled rail-mounted tricycles, and were propelled manually by a sort of rowing motion. The velocipedes were light enough to be manhandled on and off the line, and they could, if necessary, be conveyed by train.

TOWARDS CLOSURE

Despite the comparative simplicity of its operation, the Shipston-on-Stour branch could barely support a passenger service, and when, in the 1920s, rival forms of transport began to pose a major threat to such lines, the Great Western carried out an extensive review of its less profitable rural routes. In all, some 53 branches were examined in an attempt to identify where economies might be made, and for

the Shipston-on-Stour branch the following picture emerged for the year under review (1925):

	Passengers	Parcels	Goods	Totals	1924 Totals	Decrease
Shipston	£384	£553	£9,585	£10,522	£10,787	-£265
Stretton	£135	£212	£492	£839	£876	-£37
Longdon Road	£117	£108	£1,201	£1,426	£1,485	-£59

Goods traffic carried on the branch included 12,756 tons of coal and minerals, together with 7,180 tons of general merchandise. The three branch stations also handled 251 wagonloads of cattle and 2,793 cans of milk throughout 1925.

Total running costs were said to be £6,730 a year, representing 57.71 per cent of the gross traffic receipts. The locomotive department absorbed £2,676 annually, while engineering expenses, signalling, lighting, water and rates

Longdon Road station in April 1933, showing the two-siding goods yard beyond the level crossing and the 1889 curve. The left-hand siding passed through a gate to connect with the horse-worked northern section of the tramway. The horse landing platform in the 'V' of the 1889 curve and siding was provided in January 1899 at a cost of £35. The close-boarded fence on the platform screened horses from the adjacent running line. The small timber hut-like structure on the right provided cover for the weighbridge equipment only.　*L & GRP*

Looking east from the horse landing platform c.1928. Darlingscott village was hidden behind the belt of trees visible in the left distance. The Exhall private owner coal wagon belonged to one of a group of collieries in the Warwickshire coalfield from which merchants in the district generally bought supplies.　*C. L. Mowat*

View looking east towards Shipston-on-Stour from Longdon Road station on 20th July 1920.   *R. K. Cope*

amounted to £2,570 each year. Staffing costs (including 'junction staff') absorbed another £1,484, which was estimated to be 11.61 per cent of the total expenditure for 1925.

The report concluded that a small saving of £212 a year could be made if the Shipston-on-Stour branch was worked as a light railway, though it is difficult to see what scope there might have been for 'light railway' operation when the branch was already being worked as a tramway. The options considered on other lines included the introduction of auto-trains, destaffing of stations, and simplification of track and signalling, but few of these innovations would have helped the Shipston branch because it was already worked as cheaply as possible.

Inevitably, the Great Western board, when presented with the results of the 1925 survey, concluded that little could be done to effect economies. There was no alternative to closure, and from 8th July 1929 branch passenger services were replaced by a GWR bus service, leaving, however, full goods facilities at Shipston-on-Stour. In the event, the replacement bus service fared no better than the previous railway service, and the vehicles themselves were withdrawn in the following September. The Shipston branch then settled down to eke out a somewhat meagre existence as a freight-only line. In effect, the clock had been put back thirty years, and the branch was free to fulfil its original function as a bulk carrier of coal and local agricultural produce.

LOCOMOTIVES & TRAFFIC IN THE 1930s

After the First World War the sub-shed at Shipston was closed, and thereafter the line was worked by a locomotive from Worcester. Eventually in 1929 the former locomotive shed was used as garage accommodation for the GWR road transport department. This changed operating pattern presented a problem in that Shipston was 37¾ miles from Worcester, and, in view of this relatively great distance, tender engines were thereafter regularly used on the line.

Dean Goods 0-6-0s became standard motive power, their light axle loadings making them an ideal class for use on the branch which was classified as an uncoloured route. Worcester shed had around twenty of these engines.

Perhaps, surprisingly, Shipston-on-Stour still handled considerable quantities of freight traffic in the 1929-39 period. Inwards traffic included coal, building materials, agricultural machinery and general supplies, while outwards traffic consisted mainly of hay, livestock, and other agricultural products.

Privately-owned coal wagons seen on the branch included those belonging to Hutchings & Co. of Stratford-upon-Avon, together with occasional vehicles from the Coventry Colliery Company. In his book *The Stratford-upon-Avon & Midland Junction Railway*, Arthur Jordan claims that Hutchings owned thirty-five coal wagons, though it is unclear if all of these vehicles were labelled 'Stratford-upon-Avon'. Hutchings & Co. had coal wharves at Stratford, Kineton, Ettington and

Shipston-on-Stour station in 1931, looking south towards the buffer stops. Even by this date, the platform nameboard had gone, although the platform and buildings, etc., retained a neat and tidy appearance. The principal coal merchant at Shipston from at least 1904 was Hutchings & Co., who were a Stratford-on-Avon firm with depots at Shipston, Kineton and Ettington. They had a fleet of 35 private owner coal wagons and their main depot at Stratford was based at the SMJR station. The gasworks coal was also brought in by rail.

P. A. Hopkins

Shipston station viewed from the end loading dock in 1931. Constructed around 1917, the dock may have been provided to handle military traffic. This is the only picture discovered so far to feature the 2,000 gallon water tank which was removed by 1933. It can just be seen in the distance to the right of the goods shed. The oil lamps shown here were replaced by Tilley lamps in the 1930s.

P. A. Hopkins

Moreton-in-Marsh station in the 1930s, after the cessation of Shipston branch passenger services. Note the blank space on the station nameboard which had once told branches to 'Change here for the Shipston-on-Stour Tramway'.   *Lens of Sutton*

Shipston. James Atkinson, millers and bakers, of Sheep Street, Shipston, also maintained an office in Shipston goods yard, but are unlikely to have owned their own wagons.

The Great Western had, by the 1930s, invested heavily in motorised delivery vehicles, and these new lorry fleets enabled stations such as Moreton-in-Marsh and Shipston-on-Stour to serve extensive rural hinterlands. Shipston, a small town situated at a considerable distance from large centres of population, served an area extending northwards to Ilmington and Idlicote and southwards to Long Compton. Villages to the west of Shipston were served by lorries from Moreton-in-Marsh, while areas to the north and east were covered by delivery vehicles from Stratford and Banbury respectively. Further to the south, the Oxfordshire/Warwickshire border area was served by vehicles based at Hook Norton or Chipping Norton.

In 1938, a Great Western publication entitled *Towns, Villages & Outlying Works* was prepared as a guide for the benefit of railway staff wishing to know what delivery arrangements were in force at each destination. The book showed the stations to which freight or parcels should be consigned, with particular reference to rural areas. For example, if a customer turned up at Reading with a parcel for Tidmington, the staff at Reading would

find Tidmington in the book and see that it was two miles from Shipston-on-Stour and served by private carrier or GWR lorry service from Shipston station. Some villages were served from two or more stations – Tredington, for instance, was two miles from Shipston by carrier and eight miles from Stratford by GWR lorry service. In this situation the consigning station would choose the most appropriate route, depending on distance, delivery arrangements and the type of traffic.

The book of *Towns, Villages & Outlying Works* provides an interesting glimpse of how the GWR served

Branch Engine, Winter 1936/7 – WOS '2301' Group A				
4.35	Worcester	Moreton-in-Marsh	6.45	Goods
7.0	Shunt	Moreton-in-Marsh	8.0	
8.25	Moreton-in-Marsh	Honeybourne	8.43	Passenger
8.55	Honeybourne	Moreton-in-Marsh	9.21	Passenger
10.0	Moreton-in-Marsh	Campden	11.55	Goods
12/30	Campden	Moreton-in-Marsh	12/45	Goods
1/35	Moreton-in-Marsh	Shipston-on-Stour	3/5	Goods
4/5	Shipston-on-Stour	Moreton-in-Marsh	5/5	Goods
5/20	Shunt	Moreton-in-Marsh	8/35	
8/42	Moreton-in-Marsh	Evesham	9/15	Lt. Eng.
9/20	Shunt	Evesham	11/0	
11/5	Evesham	Worcester	11/25	Lt. Eng.

Moreton-in-Marsh from the footbridge c.1930, showing the branch platform (left) and the branch interchange sidings occupied by GW coaching stock. Again we can see that the 'Change for Shipston-on-Stour Tramway' had been painted out on the station nameboard. The Brunel-style timber goods shed on the right was burnt down c.1954 and later replaced by an austere red brick structure which still survives. The waiting room on the island platform was also replaced c.1962.

Lens of Sutton

Moreton-in-Marsh, looking north towards Worcester in the 1930s. In earlier times, the Stratford & Moreton tramway had crossed the OW&WR on the level between the platforms and the overbridge.   *Lens of Sutton*

Moreton-in-Marsh in July 1931, looking north. The up platform (right) retained its timber-built OW&WR type buildings for many years, but the brick-built booking office and waiting room block on the left was a Great Western addition dating from 1872-74. The station master here around 1939 was W. E. Salisbury.   *Clarence Gilbert*

This aerial view of Moreton-in-Marsh, taken on 21st May 1929, shows the Shipston-on-Stour branch diverging to the left and the old tramway terminus is visible in the foreground. A branch train can also be glimpsed alongside the branch platform.

Aerofilms

Moreton-in-Marsh, looking south during the 1930s, showing the creamery premises on the left, with three GWR Siphon J vans for milk churn traffic standing alongside the loading platform.
Lens of Sutton

The former S&M tramway terminus at Moreton-in-Marsh. These stone buildings probably accommodated horses, a weigh house and store room.
R. K. Cope

rural areas on the eve of World War Two, and using this publication as a guide it is possible to compile Table 4, showing the area served by Shipston-on-Stour station.

The Shipston delivery lorry was usually stabled overnight in the station's former engine shed, which, as mentioned, served as a road motor depot. The driver, in the 1930s was Percy Webb, a long-serving local railwayman whose grandfather, Thomas Ellis Webb, was a foreman ganger. Others employed on the branch around 1930 included PW men George Boorman, Charles Boorman and William Padbury. Sadly, Thomas Ellis Webb was killed by a goods train near Longdon Road on 3rd February 1930.

Accidents, as such, were rare on the Shipston branch after its up-grading to main line standards, but there were inevitably one or two minor derailments at Shipston and elsewhere. The most inconvenient of these incidents took place at Shipston in the early 1930s when a Dean Goods pulled out of the station before the points at the Moreton end of the yard had been properly set for the 'main line'. As a result, the 36 ton locomotive and its train of freight vehicles ploughed through the buffers at the end of the head shunt and came to rest in a vegetable patch in the nearby allotment gardens. The task of re-railing was unexpectedly difficult, but after about a week the Worcester breakdown gang were able to coax the recalcitrant locomotive back onto the rails.

WORLD WAR TWO

The outbreak of war in September 1939 failed to bring a sudden upsurge in traffic, and although most railways carried up to 50% more freight during the years of conflict, the Shipston-on-Stour branch, which served no important military or industrial installations, suffered a cut in services. Shipston goods workings were reduced to just three a week, and the intermediate stations at Stretton-on-Fosse and Longdon Road were closed to all traffic in May 1941.

Being so far from large centres of population, the branch never became a target for enemy air attacks, but when, in 1940 and 1941 the Luftwaffe bombed industrial targets in the Midlands from its bases in France, the people of Shipston could hear enemy bombers droning overhead. On 14th November 1940, for example, the 450 Luftwaffe aircraft assigned to bomb Coventry followed a navigational beam which extended from the Cherbourg Peninsula to Warwickshire, passing above Moreton-in-the-Marsh and Shipston en route to their target. On these occasions the enemy 'Path-finder' squadrons would drop flares or other incendiary devices over a wide area in an attempt to guide the main bomber force towards its target. The fires in Coventry could be seen from Shipston, while at Stratford-upon-Avon, some eighteen miles south of the target, the rumble and dull thumps of falling bombs could be clearly sensed.

As in other rural areas, Shipston and the surrounding villages played host to evacuees from nearby cities, although as the railway had been closed for eleven years, these displaced children arrived in town by road transport.

One sign that there was a war on at Shipston station was the appearance of a female lorry driver in the person of Mrs Turville. She remained at work in the area for several years after the war. Although Shipston-on-Stour was no longer used as a passenger station, it retained a proper station master, and in the early part of the war this position was filled by a Mr Austin. By the end of the war Mr Austin had, however, been replaced by Cyril Smith.

TABLE 4: GOODS AND PARCELS COLLECTION –
DELIVERY ARRANGEMENTS AT SHIPSTON-ON-STOUR

Name of Place	County	Miles from Shipston	Delivery Arrangements
Barcheston	Warwicks	1	GWR lorry service
Blackwell	Warwicks	2	GWR lorry service
Burmington	Warwicks	2	private carrier
Chelmscote	Warwicks	4	GWR lorry service
Cherrington	Warwicks	4	private carrier
Long Compton★	Warwicks	6	private carrier
Halford	Warwicks	3	private carrier
Honington	Warwicks	1¼	private carrier
Idlicote	Warwicks	3	GWR lorry/private carrier
Kirby	Warwicks	4½	private carrier
Little Wolford★	Warwicks	3½	private carrier
Middle Tysoe★	Warwicks	6	private carrier
Oxhill★	Warwicks	5	private carrier
Shipston-on-Stour	Warwicks	-	free delivery area
Stourton	Warwicks	4	private carrier
Sutton-u-Brailes	Warwicks	4	GWR lorry/private carrier
Tidmington	Warwicks	2	GWR lorry/private carrier
Tredington★	Warwicks	2	private carrier
Upper Tysoe★	Warwicks	6½	private carrier
Whatcote★	Warwicks	4	private carrier
Winderton	Warwicks	5	GWR lorry service

★ = Also served by delivery services from Moreton or other local stations

CHAPTER FIVE

THE ROUTE DESCRIBED

'Castle' class 4–6–0 No. 5063 *Earl Baldwin* entering Moreton-in-Marsh on a Worcester–Paddington train on 6th October 1951. Note the permanent way motor trolley standing in the Shipston branch bay. *P. J. Garland*

SERVING a popular tourist centre in the Gloucestershire Cotswolds, Moreton-in-Marsh station contained many relics of the Stratford & Moreton Railway. When first opened, the horse tramway had approached its southern terminus from the north-east and ended in a small yard beside the Fosse Way, with its terminal buildings more or less parallel to the road. Facilities provided in 1826 included stables, warehouses and coal wharves, and possibly also some cottages for tramway staff. Solidly constructed of local Cotswold stone, the tramway buildings looked quite at home beside Moreton's mainly 17th-century houses.

In 1853, the opening of the OW & WR main line resulted in the tramway terminus becoming isolated to the west of the new railway. The Oxford Worcester & Wolverhampton line approached Moreton-in-Marsh from the north, cutting across the existing tramway at an angle. Initially, it seems that there may have been a level crossing, enabling the tramway wagons to reach their terminus on the far side of the main line. A new connection was later installed on the up side of the OW & WR, but tramway goods wagons still had to be manhandled across the running line.

This may explain an accident that took place on 17th December 1856 when the 12.50pm Worcester to Oxford express ploughed into some 'coal wagons'. Fortunately, little damage was sustained as the OW & WR train had slowed down prior to stopping at Moreton.

The original OW & WR station had just one platform on the down side of the line – the only 2-platform passing place between Evesham and Wolvercot Junction being at Charlbury. A second platform was added at a relatively early date, and was certainly in place by 1858 when the line through Moreton was doubled. This second (ie up platform) provided a third platform face for Stratford & Moreton services, and allowed Mr Bull's passenger horse-drawn conveyance to start and terminate on the eastern side of the main line without the dangers inherent in crossing it on the level.

Brunel-type wooden buildings were provided on both platforms, the main building, on the down side, being a rectangular, gabled structure measuring approximately 32ft x 18ft. (A substantially-similar building was provided at nearby Campden station.) The up side waiting rooms were slightly

49

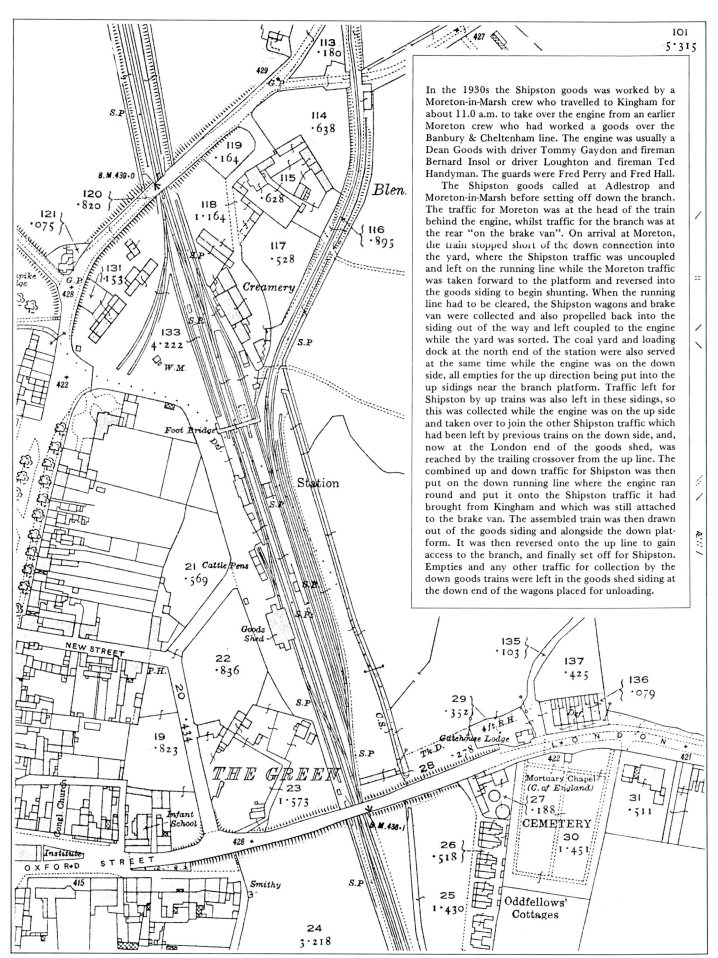

In the 1930s the Shipston goods was worked by a Moreton-in-Marsh crew who travelled to Kingham for about 11.0 a.m. to take over the engine from an earlier Moreton crew who had worked a goods over the Banbury & Cheltenham line. The engine was usually a Dean Goods with driver Tommy Gaydon and fireman Bernard Insol or driver Loughton and fireman Ted Handyman. The guards were Fred Perry and Fred Hall.

The Shipston goods called at Adlestrop and Moreton-in-Marsh before setting off down the branch. The traffic for Moreton was at the head of the train behind the engine, whilst traffic for the branch was at the rear "on the brake van". On arrival at Moreton, the train stopped short of the down connection into the yard, where the Shipston traffic was uncoupled and left on the running line while the Moreton traffic was taken forward to the platform and reversed into the goods siding to begin shunting. When the running line had to be cleared, the Shipston wagons and brake van were collected and also propelled back into the siding out of the way and left coupled to the engine while the yard was sorted. The coal yard and loading dock at the north end of the station were also served at the same time while the engine was on the down side, all empties for the up direction being put into the up sidings near the branch platform. Traffic left for Shipston by up trains was also left in these sidings, so this was collected while the engine was on the up side and taken over to join the other Shipston traffic which had been left by previous trains on the down side, and, now at the London end of the goods shed, was reached by the trailing crossover from the up line. The combined up and down traffic for Shipston was then put on the down running line where the engine ran round and put it onto the Shipston traffic it had brought from Kingham and which was still attached to the brake van. The assembled train was then drawn out of the goods siding and alongside the down platform. It was then reversed onto the up line to gain access to the branch, and finally set off for Shipston. Empties and any other traffic for collection by the down goods trains were left in the goods shed siding at the down end of the wagons placed for unloading.

Taken from 25-inch Ordnance Survey for 1922. Crown copyright reserved.

Moreton-in-Marsh, looking north on 6th October 1951.

P. J. Garland

taller than their counterparts on the opposite platform but of the same general design. These buildings were clearly assembled with the aid of pre-fabricated or semi-prefabricated 'kits', and most of the OW & WR stations had buildings of the same size and shape.

The main, down side, station building at Moreton-in-Marsh would, by analogy with neighbouring OW & WR stations, have contained just two rooms. Entering the building through double doors which faced the platform, one immediately entered a large, open plan booking hall, with a counter to the left. The right-hand end of the structure, when viewed from the platform, was occupied by the waiting room, while a small projection at the rear contained the ladies waiting room. There were apparently no public lavatories.

In later years, the substantially-similar station buildings at Campden and Adlestrop were rebuilt, their original open plan interiors being replaced by a separate booking hall/ticket office arrangement. At the same time, both stations were given proper lavatories, though it is unlikely that such alterations would have been carried out at Moreton where, as an alternative to refurbishment, the Great Western built a new station.

In 1872 the Great Western started erecting a range of new buildings beside the existing timber structure, but this work proceeded at a very slow pace and for several months the old and new station buildings stood side by side on the down platform. The original Brunelian building lasted until its replacement was finally completed in 1873.

The new station building, which was situated immediately to the south of its wooden predecessor, was a standard Great Western hip-roofed structure – indeed the building was one of the earliest examples of its type. The replacement station contained three internal divisions – the slightly recessed central portion, with its front and rear entrances, was occupied by a spacious booking hall, whilst the rooms on either side contained a ladies waiting room and ticket office respectively. An extension, containing additional staff and parcels facilities, was added in 1874, a few months after the main block had been completed. Ladies' and gents' WCs were accommodated in a small projecting block at the northern end of the structure, and a large canopy protected the entire platform frontage.

A distinctive feature of this new, standardised station design was the treatment of doors and windows, which were grouped in pairs beneath large arc-shaped concrete lintels, and in this context it is interesting to note that Radley station, which was built at the same time as the new station at Moreton, had conventional square windows, though the overall design was otherwise similar to Moreton.

The new station building was constructed of whitish-yellow bricks, with red brick quoins and window surrounds. Vitrified black bricks provided

A general view of the north end of the station, showing clearly the United Dairies factory which dominated this end of the station site. Part of the old tramway yard site can be glimpsed on the left whilst the stone overbridge dated from the opening of the OWW line in 1853, and survives to this day.   *P. J. Garland*

A close-up view of the down main starter signal situated between the up and down running lines. Because of the limited clearances between the up and down lines, the signal was provided with a centre pivoted arm.   *P. J. Garland*

Empty milk tank wagons were conveyed to Moreton in goods trains and put on the line behind the branch platform. From here they were gravitated down the slight gradient and positioned alongside the dairy for loading, after which they were gravitated to the spur beyond to await collection. The loaded tank wagons were conveyed to London on the rear of up passenger trains which, after calling at the platform (with passengers on board) were backed into the spur to collect them.

J. H. Russell

further decoration, resulting in an attractive structure. The older wooden buildings on the up platform remained in use, and Moreton therefore had two distinct types of GWR architecture – a late-Victorian main station building, and an older 'Brunel' type waiting room on the island platform.

A stylish, GWR covered footbridge had appeared by 1900, whilst at a much earlier date a standard GW signal cabin had been installed to the south of the up platform.

Moreton's goods yard was provided with a timber-built Brunelian goods shed to the south of the down platform, together with a loading dock to the north; both were served by single sidings. There were also two sharply curved sidings (known as No 1 and No 2 coal sidings) which diverged south-westwards into the old tramway yard, and may therefore have been laid on the site of former tramway sidings. A siding at the north end of the up platform served a creamery which from 1918 had its own loading platform.

Although only a small country junction, Moreton-in-Marsh was always a busy station, giving employment to a large staff of 18 men, and handling, in 1903, some 28,682 passenger bookings and 23,601 tons of freight. By 1930, goods

An unidentified 'Hall' class 4–6–0 at Moreton-in-Marsh with a Worcester–Oxford stopping train during 1947. Moreton's goods yard crane features on the left with the signal box and branch sidings on the right.

J. H. Russell

The goods shed and signal cabin at Moreton-in-Marsh. The shed was a classic Brunelian design with a central transhipment platform and twin doors in its end gables.

J. H. Moss

The branch platform on 6th October 1951 with the line to Shipston curving away sharply to the right. Besides serving the platforms, the footbridge continued right across the railway because it maintained a public right of way to a footpath on the east of the station. By this date there were very few of the GW 6-wheel milk Siphons on the right still in service.   *P. J. Garland*

A passenger's view of the branch curving away from Moreton station in 1947, with Todenham Road Crossing keeper's cottage in the distance.   *J. H. Russell*

Todenham Road Level Crossing c.1947. After the withdrawal of passenger services, the level crossings were opened by the fireman and closed by the guard.   *J. H. Russell*

tonnage had exceeded 36,000 tons but passenger bookings had fallen to just 20,672 tickets.

Shipston trains departed from the eastern side of the station, making use of the island platform that presumably dated from tramway days. The branch diverged to the right from a point halfway along the platform, trains for Shipston departing slowly with flanges screeching on the sharp curve. As they started to climb at 1 in 94, the single track swung round to the left, and, having executed an 'S'-bend, passed a 'Limit of Shunt' notice. The first level crossing was immediately beyond; known officially as Todenham Road Crossing, it was usually referred to by train crews as White's Crossing after Mrs Kate White, who manned the gates. Her red brick crossing keeper's cottage could be seen to the right as trains crawled past at a regulation 4 mph.

These brick-built crossing keeper's cottages were, apart from the wooden station buildings at Shipston, Longdon Road and Stretton-on-Fosse, the most characteristic structures on the Shipston-on-Stour branch. There were nine in all and, although all were superficially similar, no two were identical in terms of detail. They were constructed of red brick, with grey slate roofs and slightly-arched window and door

apertures, but there was considerable variation in the way that doors and windows were arranged, most examples having blank walls facing the track, with entrances and windows in the gable ends. The main doorways were offset to one side, and each cottage had a small slated porch. A window to the left (or right) of the front door illuminated the living room, and there was another window in the apex of the gable. Some of the rear gable walls had twinned windows, and there was usually a four-flue chimney in the wall adjacent to the track.

Most of the cottages conformed to the same basic plan, but Shipston Road Crossing had a slightly larger house with distinctive half-hipped gables. The cottages ceased to be used as crossing cottages after the cessation of passenger services in 1929, but the former gate keepers remained in their houses for many years thereafter, and at least two – Mrs Gertrude Parnell and Mrs Kate White – were still living in their houses in the early 1960s.

Having safely cleared Todenham Road Crossing, branch trains were able to reach their maximum permitted speed of 20 mph, and labouring up the prevailing 1 in 106 gradient, the short, 'mixed' formations soon rattled past the Moreton fixed distant. To the left, a

A Shipston to Moreton goods approaching the Moreton–Todenham Road Level Crossing on 4th September 1948, headed by Dean Goods No. 2551. The Moreton fixed distant can just be seen in the distance.
R. E. Tustin

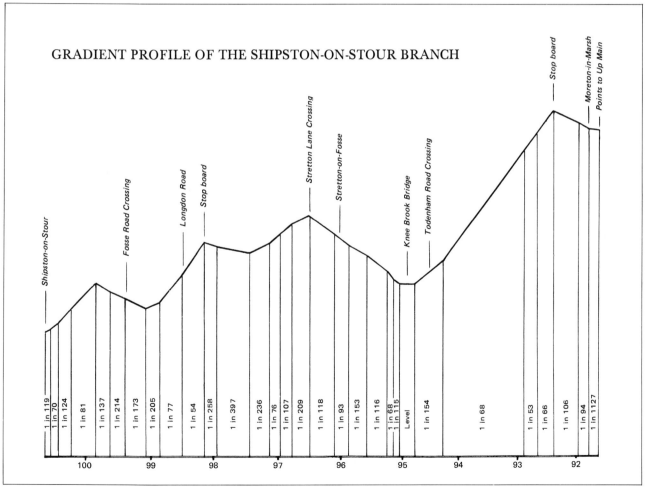

GRADIENT PROFILE OF THE SHIPSTON-ON-STOUR BRANCH

Having crossed Todenham Road Level Crossing, the branch ran through deep cuttings, with the Fosse Way running parallel to the left. The small hut visible beside one of the telegraph poles contained a telephone which could be used by permanent way men. Known as 'Hut No. 1', this tiny structure was 1 mile 60 chains from Moreton-in-Marsh. April 1933.

D. S. Barrie/L & GRP

picturesque Cotswold stone cottage beside the line had once been a tramway store. Reaching its summit the route then began to fall on descending gradients of 1 in 66, followed by a short section as steep as 1 in 53; the actual summit was marked by a stop board which informed 'all down goods and mineral trains to stop and pin down brakes'.

With the present A429 road running parallel to the left, the railway entered a deep cutting and passed beneath a minor road bridge before curving onto a more easterly heading.

Falling on a long 1 in 68 descending gradient, the single track passed under a second road overbridge and then struck out across open country, with the village of Lower Lemington partially hidden by a belt of trees on the right-hand side of the line. Still descending, trains slowed to their customary 4 mph prior to reaching Lemington Lane Crossing (1 mile 48 chains from Moreton).

Curving imperceptibly onto a more northerly heading, the route continued to descend at 1 in 68 past

C. F. Klapper, C. L. Mowat and C. R. Clinker beneath the first overbridge along the branch, during an exploratory visit in April 1933. The sports jacket, Oxford bags and V-necked pullovers were very much the look of the 1930s undergraduates. *D. S. Barrie/L & GRP*

The view from the bridge seen in the previous photo, looking south, on 31st August 1940.

H. C. Casserley

Longdon Road station, facing Moreton-in-Marsh in 1947. After the cessation of passenger services in 1929, both Stretton-on-Fosse and Longdon Road stations were staffed by Grade 1 porters, but, with the meagre freight traffic, both intermediate stations closed to freight traffic on 1st June 1941. In 1942-3 the late-turn porter from Moreton-in-Marsh covered porter's duties at Stretton-on-Fosse. Porter Archie Warren recalled cycling there on Tuesdays and Thursdays. On Mondays, Wednesdays and Fridays when the goods train ran, he travelled down with the guard. Any parcels were dealt with in the booking office, but there was hardly anything. "I never saw a soul and to relieve the boredom I often used to walk along the track." When the train returned, he operated the level crossing gates for the crew and returned to Moreton in the van. *J. H. Russell*

Oldborough Farm. Slowing to 4 mph once again at Todenham Lane Level Crossing (2 miles 64 chains), trains soon reached the Knee Brook (pronounced 'Nay') where a small bridge carried the railway across the stream and into Warwickshire.

The Knee Brook Bridge was, like many of the other bridges along the route to Shipston, an interesting structure which showed clear signs of its origins as a tramway bridge. It had two spans, one across the actual Knee Brook and the other for the benefit of local farmers. There was much timber and wrought ironwork in its structure, and it is assumed that such materials were relics of Rastrick's original bridge.

The section of line on either side of the Knee Brook was the only level section on the entire branch. Beyond, the route climbed towards Stretton-on-Fosse on a succession of adverse gradients, the steepest section being a short stretch of 1 in 68.

Running northwards on a low embankment, trains crossed a farm track by means of an overbridge, and, with rolling hills visible on both sides, approached Stretton-on-Fosse, the first intermediate station.

Situated some 4 miles 12 chains from Moreton-in-Marsh, Stretton-on-Fosse was a small, single-platform station with a tiny, prefabricated building, similar to others erected at various places throughout the GWR system during the 1880s (other examples being Littleton & Badsey on the Oxford-Worcester main line, and Upwey Junction, near Weymouth). These buildings were essentially low-cost structures, suitable

for use as subsidiary accommodation at large stations (eg porter's rooms, waiting rooms, and so on) or as basic office/passenger accommodation at very small stations; the design was distinguished by its prominent, external timber framing, which produced a 'Tudor' look. Any architectural pretentions were, however, severely compromised by an array of stovepipe chimneys, which protruded starkly through the flat, sloping roof of the station, producing a distinctly 'Emmett' appearance.

Although Stretton-on-Fosse did not appear in the timetables as a station when the line was re-opened in July 1889, passenger trains called by request at the nearby Golden Cross Inn until the station proper was completed in November 1892.

The goods yard was served by a single, dead-end siding which could accommodate about six short wheelbase wagons, and was worked from a 2-lever ground frame locked by a key attached to the wooden train staff.

Because the siding trailed in the down direction, it was normally served by Shipston-bound trains. However, south-bound trains were permitted to stop short of the siding in order that loaded wagons could be detached. The locomotive and passenger vehicle(s) would then draw forward into the platform and, after the guard had operated the points, the wagons were gravitated into the goods yard. This operation took place only when it was necessary to send vehicles from Shipston to Stretton-on-Fosse, and appendices to the GWR working timetables warned that 'great care' was needed 'when gravitating wagons from the train into the siding'. Otherwise wagons for Moreton were picked up by down trains and taken on to Shipston and worked back through Stretton to Moreton-in-Marsh on an up train.

The passenger platform was about 170ft long, and a small cottage was provided for the benefit of railway staff and their families. Ancillary equipment included a single platform seat, two nameboards (later reduced to just one) and a selection of porter's barrows. In the Edwardian era these included one 4-wheeled trolley, a 2-wheeler, and an archaic wheelbarrow-type single wheeler.

To the east, the three-storey, red brick Golden Cross Hotel dominated the entire station. A symmetrical building

Another view of the derelict station at Stretton-on-Fosse taken in 1947, showing piles of sleepers on the platform and rails placed in the '4 foot'.   *J. H. Russell*

Close-up view of the pump trolley stored in the siding at Stretton-on-Fosse in 1947.
J. H. Russell

Stretton-on-Fosse, looking north towards Shipston during the 1930s, with the Golden Cross Hotel on the right. This building would have acted as a kind of 'station' in tramway days, just as coaching inns played a part in contemporary road transport. The 2-lever siding ground frame can be seen alongside the siding turnout on the right.   *Lens of Sutton*

of classical proportions, this Georgian-style inn was a notable survivor from the tramway era. Similar buildings are frequently found alongside canal tow paths.

Small, sleeper-built platelayers' huts were provided at regular intervals along the route of the line, and there was a typical example at Stretton-on-Fosse. Situated on the up side, and to the south of the passenger platform, this small building was fabricated from old sleepers. There was a tall, brick-built chimney stack at the rear, and a door opened into the snug interior of the hut where, in winter, a roaring fire provided warmth and comfort for ganger Webb and his permanent way men.

It is likely that when the Shipston-on-Stour branch was re-opened as a passenger-carrying line in 1889, the lineside platelayers' huts would have conformed to the same basic design, but in later years, when wind, rain, fires, and other eventualities had taken their toll, some of the huts were rebuilt with different roof profiles, taller chimneys or other refinements. At Stretton-on-Fosse, the original PW hut was eventually joined by a slightly larger, gabled structure which stood beside the original and provided increased storage and messing facilities.

Departing from Stretton-on-Fosse, trains passed over a gated level crossing which carried the A429 – the Fosse Way – across the railway. Beyond, the route curved north-westwards, and with the village of Stretton-on-Fosse visible away to the left, trains entered a surprisingly deep cutting which marked the site of Campden Road Tunnel. Just before this

The level crossing at Stretton-on-Fosse on 31st August 1952. Note the overlapping gates caused by the width of the Fosse Way Road at this point. The former station master's house on the right was extended in January 1903 with an additional bedroom and wash house added to the south end of the building at a cost of £86.

P. J. Garland

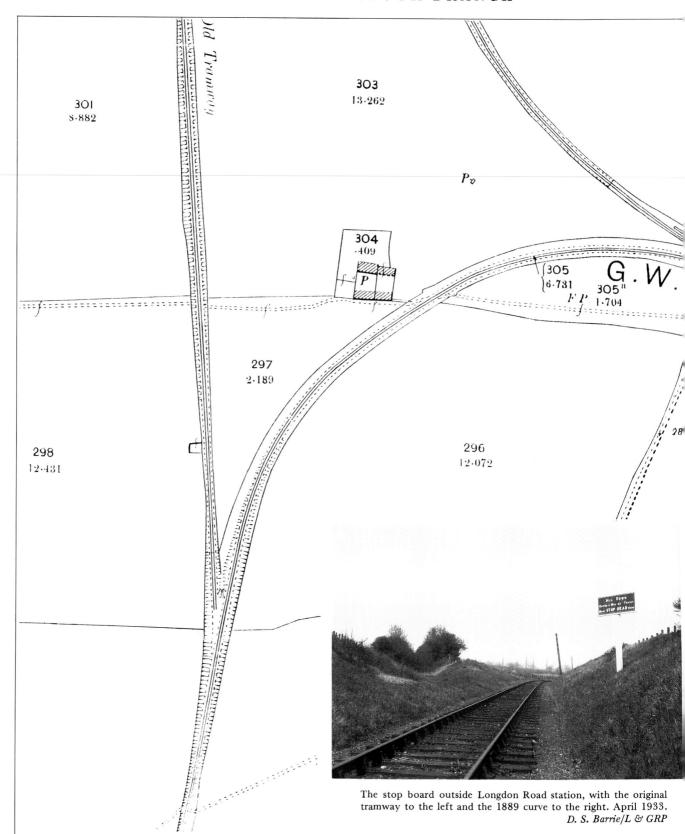

301
8·882

303
13·262

Old Tramway

P_v

304
·409

P

305
6·731

305ª
1·704

F.P.

G.W.

297
2·189

298
12·431

296
12·072

28

The stop board outside Longdon Road station, with the original tramway to the left and the 1889 curve to the right. April 1933.
D. S. Barrie/L & GRP

Taken from 25-inch Ordnance Survey for 1902. Crown copyright reserved.

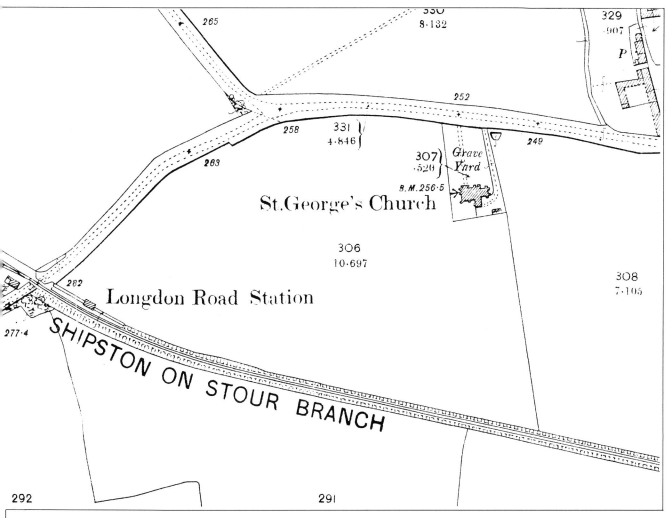

St.George's Church

Longdon Road Station

SHIPSTON ON STOUR BRANCH

cutting, the line crossed Stretton Lane on the level, the crossing being known as 'Stretton Road' or 'Parnell's Crossing' after Mrs Gertrude Parnell, who operated the gates here from 1916 until the withdrawal of passenger services in 1929. Mrs Parnell had moved to the area when her first husband, Fred Badnell, was transferred, on health grounds, from his job as signalman at Kidlington, near Oxford. He died just eighteen months later, but his wife stayed at Stretton Road as crossing keeper and later remarried.

Accelerating through the deep cutting, northbound trains rumbled beneath Campden Road bridge, and with the sound of the labouring branch engine leaving no doubt that the general direction was now upwards, the single line suddenly emerged onto an embankment that was pierced, at one point, by a brick-built underbridge.

Campden Road bridge was always referred to locally as 'The Tunnel' or 'The Tunnel Bridge', and it is interesting to find that this substantial structure was the subject of an amusing anecdote. It seems that when the bridge was under construction in the 1880s, the navvies and bricklayers decided to place bets on what would be the very first

vehicle to cross the completed brick span. Some argued that a horse and cart would be the first conveyance to cross, while others suggested that the first crossing would be made by a carriage and pair – few however could have guessed that the first object to cross the bridge was 'an Italian organ-grinder and his monkey'!

Now heading in a northerly direction, the route ran parallel to a minor road for the next mile or so, curving first left and then right in a great arc which carried the railway through a full 90 degree turn.

Until its rebuilding in the 1880s, the main line had continued straight on towards Ilmington, where, to reach Shipston-on-Stour, the horse-drawn trains had reversed onto the branch via a trailing connection. When the branch was re-opened in 1889 however, Shipston trains used the new curve which left the old line immediately north of the level crossing to Longdon Manor, and continued for approximately 600 yards to rejoin the tramway route at Longdon Road. This new curve formed the third side of a triangle, though it is believed that all services used the direct line via Longdon Road after 1889. The original 'main line' remained *in situ* for

An evocative view of Dean Goods 0–6–0 No. 2458 standing on the heavily graded Longdon curve with a southbound Moreton-in-Marsh goods train on 2nd July 1953. This picture was taken from the brake van while the guard closed the Longdon Road Level Crossing gates behind.

Collection R. S. Carpenter

The somewhat semi-derelict station at Longdon Road, looking south to Moreton-in-Marsh in 1947. Like Stretton-on-Fosse, the former station building and goods lock-up were removed by 1952. *J. H. Russell*

many years, and was still shown on 1902 Ordnance Survey maps, albeit severed at the southern end. A glance to the left revealed the tramway disappearing into an overgrown cutting. Nearby a stop board warned all down goods and mineral trains to 'Stop Dead' prior to descending the 1 in 54 incline towards Longdon Road station.

Tightly-curved and steeply-graded, Longdon Curve represented a formidable challenge for heavily-laden up trains, and it was perhaps fortunate for the loco crews that the Shipston-on-Stour branch did not carry significant freight traffic. There were, nevertheless, occasional goods trains, and in the early days a freight service ran 'as required' from Shipston to Moreton at 12.15pm; in practice this service seems to have been necessary on Shipston sale days, and in this context it is said that long cattle trains had to be stopped and divided at Longdon Road before they could negotiate the curve.

With wheel flanges screeching in protest, down trains cautiously rounded Longdon curve, passing, on the left, a small farmyard complete with barns and outhouses. Having

safely negotiated the curve, the trains entered Longdon Road station (6 miles 54 chains) from the west.

Longdon Road (for Ilmington) was very similar to Stretton-on-Fosse, with the same 'Emmett' style wooden building on a single, short platform, situated on the down side of the line. A corrugated-iron shed provided additional accommodation for parcels, bicycles and similar items, and there were two sharply curving sidings to the west of a level crossing which bisected the station. One of these was a short goods siding used mainly by local coal merchants, but the other was the post-1889 tramway main line.

It is interesting to note that at least some traffic was worked northwards onto the tramway until around 1900 though not on any regular basis, and possibly unofficially. These isolated movements of individual wagons ceased for good in 1917, when all remaining rails between Longdon Road and Stratford were lifted for scrap.

It was, perhaps, at its intermediate stations that the Shipston-on-Stour branch exhibited its true 'light railway' character. The weigh house at Longdon Road, for example, was a tiny

Looking east from the former horse landing at Longdon Road, facing Shipston-on-Stour in 1947, with the derelict sidings and the weigh machine hut on the left. The sidings were removed by 1952 but the former station master's house on the right and the one at Stretton-on-Fosse still survive today as private dwellings.   *J. H. Russell*

Close-up of the 4-lever ground frame in 1947, which controlled the siding points and facing point locks at Longdon Road. The relaying notice board in front of the brick and timber-built PW hut recorded the date for rail renewal. These boards, common on the GW system up to the 1930s, gradually disappeared over the following twenty years or so. In this instance the left-hand column of the inscription indicated relaid secondhand 01 section rails in 1917, whilst the right-hand side recorded the provision of 00.12 section rails in 1924. The use of secondhand PW materials on branch lines where traffic was light was a common practice.   *J. H. Russell*

The guard of an up freight train closing the gates at Fosse Road Crossing, near Shipston-on-Stour. Shipston Road Crossing can be glimpsed in the distance. 2nd July 1953.

Collection R. S. Carpenter

wooden hut, barely large enough to cover the weighing machine. Neither Longdon Road nor Stretton-on-Fosse had any goods sheds, yard cranes or cattle pens, and they were in effect merely staffed halts.

Longdon Road and Stretton-on-Fosse were both lit by simple oil lamps, the lamps consisting, in each case, of glass lanterns on fluted iron posts. Old photographs suggest that, when first opened, Stretton-on-Fosse was equipped with very simple, timber-posted lamps, but these were later replaced by standard GW iron lamp posts. Longdon Road had four lamps on its platform, and a fifth was provided beside the level crossing gates.

Curiously, there was no Longdon village at the end of 'Longdon Road', and the lane that ran southwards beyond the level crossing eventually led to Stretton-on-Fosse. The station should really have been called 'Darlingscott' after the hamlet of that name, but the GWR, displaying a patrician disregard for the wishes of ordinary folk in these matters, named the station after a nearby manor house.

From Longdon Road, the single-track branch continued eastwards with open fields to the right and the straggling hamlet of Darlingscott away to the left. In the west, Ilmington Downs formed an attractive backdrop, the rounded, grassy flanks imparting an air of seclusion to the entire scene. Nearer at hand, St George's Church, Darlingscott, could be seen from the railway, and although its fabric and furnishings contained nothing of real antiquity, the sight of this tiny Anglican church standing alone in a grassy meadow added much to an already picturesque rural scene.

Falling at 1 in 77, the railway ran in an almost dead straight line through green fields which bore the curious, corrugated imprint of medieval ploughlands. Passing Darlingscott Green Level Crossing (7 miles 4 chains), trains coasted downhill for a further quarter of a mile, and, having crossed a small stream, the route climbed at 1 in 173 towards the next level crossing at Fosse Road (7 miles 57 chains). Darlingscott & Shipston Road Crossing was only 15 chains further on. Here, a minor road crossed the line diagonally, and the single level crossing gates were swung through almost 180 degrees when the crossing was opened or closed to road traffic.

Entering further cuttings, the line surmounted a miniature summit before descending towards Shipston on a 1 in 81

Shipston Road Level Crossing, viewed from the brake van of the same train while the guard fastened the gates on 2nd July 1953. This picture captures something of the atmosphere of the rural branch line scene during the early 1950s. The telephone lines appear to have been receiving some attention from GPO engineers, whose small, dark-green-painted Ford vans were so common around the roads of Britain at this time. There were no gatekeepers after the withdrawal of passenger services in 1929, but these gatekeepers' cottages still survive along the route of the branch as private dwellings.

Collection R. S. Carpenter

A general view of the terminus from the throat of the yard approach in April 1933, showing the former passenger station in the distance, with the goods shed, the large cattle dock and the roof of the former loco shed on the right. A 2,000 gallon pillar tank had formerly stood immediately beyond the PW gangers hut. The area of land behind the hut was used for allotments. *L & GRP*

gradient. Emerging from another cutting, the branch turned slightly to the left before curving unexpectedly rightwards, and negotiating another 90 degree turn into the terminus.

Shipston-on-Stour station was 8 miles 75 chains from Moreton-in-Marsh. It was, in many ways, a classic GW branch terminus with all the usual facilities, including a goods shed, cattle dock, end-loading bay and engine shed. No signal box was needed as the branch was always worked on the 'One Engine in Steam' principle.

The station building was, as mentioned earlier, a prefabricated structure with a projecting canopy. Like Stretton-on-Fosse and Longdon Road, the structure was utterly basic (at least by Victorian standards) though it was considerably larger than the other two stations, and had a hipped, slated roof. The station layout was controlled by two ground frames, which were strategically sited at either end of the 700ft run-round loop, and locked by a key attached to the single line train staff.

Shipston-on-Stour's corrugated-iron goods shed was an interesting, if somewhat ugly architectural specimen, with a boldly-curved roof profile. It stood on a solid brick base, and incorporated a two-storey office which extended from the southern gable. The east wall was pierced by four windows, grouped in two pairs, and the western wall contained another pair of windows and a large door for road vehicles. This vehicular entrance was protected by a

This stop board instructing footplate crews of approaching trains probably dated from the cessation of passenger services in 1929.
H. F. Wheeller

The provision of an engine shed and water supply at Shipston was evidently an afterthought, surviving internal correspondence from 22nd October 1888 revealing 'No provision was made in the "Tramway Estimate" for any water supply as it was proposed to erect the engine shed at Moreton where there is already a supply'. The water at Shipston was not suitable for locomotives, and in an earlier letter to William Dean on 9th October 1888, G. Armstrong wrote 'the water which is provided should only be used for washing out, and filling up the boiler after washing out. There is good water at Moreton and the engine should always fill up at that station'. A 17ft deep well was dug outside the front of the shed on the north side of the track, water being raised by a steam elevator in the well, powered by steam from the branch engine via a pipe coupled in place of one of the whistles. In the circumstances, the GWR's standard 3,000 gallon pillar tank was regarded as 'somewhat large for Shipston', so a 2,000 gallon tank which was 'in stock' at Swindon was provided instead. Another letter to Dean from the Manager's office at Swindon said 'Would you please ask Mr. Robottom [engineers office at Wolverhampton] to keep the brickwork basement of the pillar tank which we are sending him 18 inches above rail level or it will not be high enough for the swinging jib crane to go over our saddle tank engines. The old pattern tank we are sending is 11ft 6in from foot of pillar to centre of jib crane, whereas our new pillar tanks are 13ft 0in from foot to centre of jib, so that the 18in elevation of the base will put it the right height'. Dean proposed the tank should be sited on the ramp at the northern end of the station platform whereas Mr. Robottom suggested it was erected at the opposite end of the platform by the toe of the engine release points, but in the end it was erected alongside the run-round loop between the yard entry and headshunt points. The brick-built engine shed had internal dimensions of 41ft long and 16ft wide, with heights to the wall plate and ridge of 13ft 6in and 21ft 3in. A 30ft 9in long pit was provided inside the shed but, perhaps surprisingly, there was no other outside pit for disposal, nor, for that matter, was any coal stage provided, a note on the official shed document for 1896 recording 'Engine coaled from wagon'.

J. H. Russell

The course of the line heading out to Moreton. The headshunt spur of the run-round loop was the spot for a spectacular derailment during the early 1930s. Apparently, the daily goods train, headed by a Dean Goods 0−6−0, was pulling out of the station, manned by a crew who were notorious for 'singing and larking about'. Unfortunately, the points at the Moreton end of the yard had not been set for the main line, and the train set off along the short headshunt spur. By the time the loco crew had realised what was happening, it was too late. The locomotive ploughed through the buffer stop and into the allotment gardens at the end of the yard. It was stranded there for a week or so until a breakdown gang from Worcester came to rerail it. The engine attracted a number of schoolboys who went to the station in the evenings when nobody was around, to play on the footplate. This photograph was taken c.1949.   *M. E. J. Deane*

Another view of Shipston engine shed on 27th August 1936.   *W. A. Camwell*

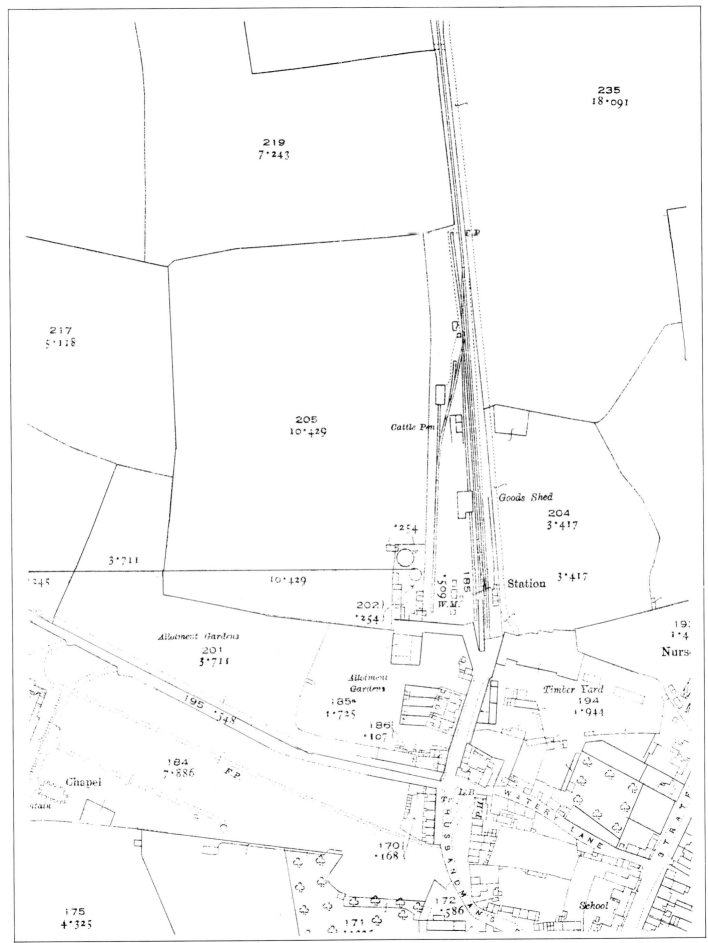

235
18·091

219
7·243

217
5·118

205
10·429

F.P.

Cattle Pen

Goods Shed
204
3·417

·254

3·711

·345

10·429

202)
·254

185
·509
W.M.

Station
3·417

19:
i·4

Nurs

201
3·711

Allotment Gardens

195 ·348

184
7·886

Allotment
Gardens
185ª
1·725

186
·107

Timber Yard
194
1·944

Chapel

F.P.

L.B
P.H

tain

170
·168

HUSBANDMAN

WATER LANE

STRAT

175
4·325

172
·586

School

171
·

Taken from 25-inch Ordnance Survey for 1923. Crown copyright reserved.

A similar view showing the large cattle dock which saw considerable use on the occasions of the Shipston Fatstock Show. However, Harold Hall, who served as a porter at Shipston during the 1930s, could not remember the cattle pens being used.   *M. E. J. Deane*

The points leading to the goods shed road and back siding were combined to form a three-way point (see page 104) but this was replaced during the station layout alterations c.1917 when the short spur near the loco shed, which held the old tender used for water storage, was also removed. The loop entry crossover was controlled by a two-lever ground frame situated behind the photographer, and similarly the engine release crossover was also worked from a ground frame. The gasometer of the Shipston-on-Stour Gas Light & Coke Co. can be seen to the left of the engine shed roof. This picture was taken on 31st August 1952.   *H. F. Wheeller*

projecting corrugated-iron canopy. Internally, the shed contained a loading platform and a small hand crane.

In contrast to its austere goods shed (which may have been a later addition), Shipston's brick-built engine shed was a stylish structure with four recessed bays, built to a standard Great Western design. A characteristic GWR 2,000 gallon pillar tank was also provided, but in practice locos took water at Moreton-in-Marsh, and the Shipston tank seems to have been used mainly for boiler washouts (or emergencies).

In physical terms, the terminus remained more or less unaltered for many years, and the track layout in use in 1960 was little different to that provided at the time of opening apart from the removal of the engine shed siding and the provision of an end loading dock around 1917. A further

Shipston-on-Stour goods shed in the 1940s, showing the standard GWR loading gauge, and the two grounded van bodies which provided warehousing.
J. H. Russell

A roadside view of the goods shed, c.1949, showing again the two grounded vehicles provided for warehousing about ten years earlier. The inside-framed van body was probably of Taff Vale Railway origin, while the other vehicle appears to have been a Dean 40ft bogie passenger brake van. The GWR motor lorry which replaced a horse-drawn dray, was initially kept in the disused loco shed, but by the 1940s it was simply parked under the goods shed canopy.
J. H. Moss

The austere goods shed was constructed in corrugated iron on a brick base and secured with sliding doors across the rail and road entrances. Internally, the shed deck, equipped with the usual 30 cwt crane, was accessible by means of steps immediately inside the rail entrances. There was a checker's desk on the deck at the south end of the central cart bay and, in the south corner, a weighing machine. A flight of steps against the office wall led up to a lock-up above the office, but by the 1930s it was hardly used. The projecting office at this end of the building was equipped with a wall-mounted desk across the end wall under the window. This was used by the station master, clerk and the checker. The wall at the back of the office was fitted with shelves and a cupboard. This photograph was taken c.1949.   *J. H. Moss*

GOODS TRAFFIC IN THE 1930s

COAL

One of the coal merchants was Berrow & Curry of Cherrington, who had taken over another local company during the early 1930s. The two partners each drove a lorry, delivering mainly to the country districts. They did not have an office or wharfage in the yard but stored supplies at their home. They also ran a bus service from Shipston to Stratford on market days, calling at the villages.

The other coal merchant in the 1930s was Hutchings, a Stratford-based company with an office next to the weighbridge in the station yard. They also rented wharfage beside their office. They had their own wagons which were painted dark blue with white lettering. They mostly served the town, where deliveries were made with a horse and cart, but they also had a lorry for country runs. Their yard man was Tom Saunders who lived in the cottages in Station Road. Hutchings were also agents for Hudsons' sacks which were stored in an old office on the town side of the weighbridge.

Each company received an average of about 2-3 wagons a week.

Coal also arrived for the local gas works, which was situated at the back of the goods yard, supplies being unloaded by the Gas Company's employees. Coke from the works seems to have been sold locally rather than sent out by rail.

TIMBER

About two Macaw loads of rough-cut timber arrived each week for timber merchant Mayo who had premises in Station Road. The wood, mostly elm, was felled all over the country by Mayo's men, often in the clearance of storm damage. It was unloaded using Mayo's own self-propelled crane, which ran over from the timber yard.

Mayos made pit props which were loaded loose on their sides in open wagons. Many of these were sent to Cannock Chase Colliery. They also made coffin boards which were loaded flat and sent out in Open C wagons to large centres such as Bristol, Birmingham and London. 'Green' boards were not sheeted, but seasoned and prepared boards were sheeted twice, one sheet being tucked over the boards inside the wagon and another one or two sheets secured conventionally over the wagon.

ROADSTONE

Warwickshire County Council received wagonloads of stone chippings for road improvements in the area, supervised by their surveyor, a Mr. Knight. They also received barrels of bitumen which were taken to the council yard in the town. Collection and site deliveries were made by the council's own men.

Shipston-on-Stour goods yard, looking north, and showing the standard GW weigh house (left) and Hutchings' coal office. The weighbridge was also used by the public who were apparently charged slightly more than rail users. The office was equipped with a table and chair which were used by the checker who kept the wagon books.

M. E. J. Deane

minor alteration also carried out around this time concerned the replacement of a 3-way point at the station throat with two conventional turnouts at the entry to the goods yard and run-round loop.

In tramway days, the line had terminated amid green fields on the northern edge of Shipston, but the presence of cheap bulk transport facilities clearly attracted modest industrial development in the form of a timber yard and a gas works.

These installations were nevertheless small in scale and did not in any way detract from the rural atmosphere of Shipston or its little station.

The terminus was conveniently sited in relation to the town, and visitors, having arrived by train could easily walk to the town centre with its Georgian shops and Victorian church. Historically, Shipston was part of Worcestershire though surrounding parishes were in Warwickshire. The

A panoramic view of the terminus facing the buffers in 1947. The group of three buildings on the right consisted of Hudson's sacks office, GW weighbridge office, and Hutchings' coal office on the right. This view also shows the yard gates. *J. H. Russell*

DAILY ROUTINE IN THE 1930s

During the 1930s, there were just four members of staff at Shipston: Jack Bourne, station master; Bill Hudson, checker; Harold Hall, porter; and a succession of relief clerks. Jack Bourne was a single man who lodged with Mr. and Mrs. Pratley in the High Street. He was responsible for all the stations on the branch and spent much of his time preparing consignment notes, all the accounts and the four-weekly summaries. Bill Hudson was a local man who lived in Telegraph Street. He labelled all the wagons, dealt with demurrage charges and generally worked in conjunction with the clerk and station master. Harold Hall lived in Bledington and lodged at Shipston during the week in one of the cottages near the station. He went home on Saturdays, taking the goods train to Moreton and catching a passenger train from there to Kingham, travelling with his bicycle which he used for the remainder of the journey home. On Sunday evenings he cycled the whole way back to Shipston.

Harold Hall's duty began with unlocking and opening the yard gates at 8.0 a.m. each morning and sweeping the weighbridge ready for use. He assisted the checker as required but his main work was concentrated in the parcels office in the station building.

Smalls traffic was sent from Hockley each day and was usually unloaded in the goods shed at Moreton-in-Marsh and taken to Shipston by lorry. However, sometimes there was sufficient traffic for Shipston that the truck was worked down the branch and unloaded in Shipston goods shed.

The lorry, based at Moreton, also delivered parcels traffic and arrived at Shipston between 9.0 and 10.0 a.m. The smalls traffic, primarily supplies for the shops, was unloaded at the goods shed and the lorry also called at the station building, backing up the platform ramp to deliver parcels and collect any brought in the previous day.

Harold and Bill made sure they had their lunch promptly at midday so they were ready for the arrival of the daily goods train at 1.0 p.m., when they were needed to help the guard with the shunting.

When the train arrived, it went into the platform road, and, after the engine had run round, it was drawn out and propelled into the back road. The brake van was then put back into the platform where the outgoing train was assembled on to it. By this time, there were rarely more than about a dozen wagons either way, so there was little congestion to impede the placing of goods shed and coal traffic in the desired positions, although wagons in the back siding might have to be rearranged to enable coal for the gas company to be placed against the buffer stops alongside the works for unloading. During the afternoon, Harold assisted wherever required but his primary concern was the receipt of any parcels brought up to the station. All the staff went home when the station closed at 5.0 p.m.

J. H. Russell

Another 1947 view of Shipston-on-Stour station, this time looking north, and again showing the neglected trackwork of this rundown outpost.

Another view of Shipston-on-Stour station in 1947. The accommodation within this wooden structure is believed to have been, from left to right, the gentlemen's lavatory, ladies' lavatory and waiting room, general waiting room, and the office. In later years, the office was used for the booking and storage of parcels and was provided with a weighing machine. The building measured approximately 46ft x 14½ft at ground level.
J. H. Russell

town's population barely exceeded 2,000, and its name had originally signified the 'Sheep Town'. Perversely, the OW & WR insisted on spelling it 'Shipstone', probably to prevent confusion with Shipton-under-Wychwood.

Shipston-on-Stour had a staff of four, reduced, in later years to just two or three. The earliest station master was Charles Mace, who supervised the tramway wharf throughout the 1870s and early 1880s. Later, around 1900, the station master was Mr A. H. Smith, but he was replaced, in the early years of the present century, by George C. Collier. In 1908, Mr Collier moved to Worcester to take up a new appointment as chief booking clerk, and in his place Mr G. W. Lane became Shipston's station master.

There was a further change in 1910 when Mr Lane left Shipston-on-Stour to become station master at Charlbury, and Frederick C. Buckingham (formerly a goods clerk at Chipping Norton) came to Shipston as station master. Mr Buckingham remained for seven years, but in 1917 he left to take up a new position at Much Wenlock, and Ezra Greenway, the district relief station master at Worcester, was sent to Shipston as a replacement.

Other staff employed at the station in the years before World War One included guards E. Hudson and George Salisbury and the crossing keepers at Darlingscott Road and Fosse Road crossings who, for administrative purposes, came under the supervision of the Shipston-on-Stour station master.

Some GW employees, such as Mr Salisbury, were content to remain in one place for most of their working lives, but

The single point lever that operated the engine release points at the southern end of the platform.
J. H. Moss

Close-up of the former tramway gate at Longdon Road station on the occasion of a visit in April 1933 by (from left to right) C. R. Clinker, C. L. Mowat and C. F. Klapper, as well as D. S. Barrie who took this photograph. Notice how the track finished abruptly at the foot of the gate. The tramway beyond to Stratford was mostly lifted during 1917-18 when numerous GWR low-revenue branch lines were recovered for the 'war effort'. The pile of coal behind the men indicates the presence of a resident coal merchant in the yard at that time.

D. S. Barrie/L & GRP

other, perhaps more ambitious men made frequent changes to gain promotion. The pages of the *Great Western Magazine* provide a glimpse of the many staff changes at stations such as Shipston-on-Stour. In May 1913, for example, porter-guard J. W. Payne left Shipston to become a shunter at Evesham, while in the same month L. Warner, a lampman from Kingham, moved to Shipston as a shunter guard.

Returning to Longdon Road, it would be appropriate to look in greater detail at the long-abandoned northern section of the S & M Tramway. As already mentioned, one of two sidings in Longdon Road goods yard provided a tenuous connection with the tramway until 1900 (and perhaps until 1917) and wagons bound for destinations north of Longdon Road were collected from the goods yard and hauled westwards, through a mysterious-looking gate, onto the tramway beyond.

From here these wagons, which may have carried the occasional unofficial passenger on market days, were taken through a shallow cutting to the site of Ilmington Junction, where an attractive, gabled cottage known as 'Junction House' recalled the days when this isolated spot had been a central point on the horse-worked tramway.

From Junction House the line crossed a minor road and headed due north, through Blackwell Bushes. The large

A close-up view of Junction cottage taken from the site of the Moreton line facing Stratford. The gate in the foreground marks the spot where the former Moreton line crossed the lane. A similar gate existed to the right and behind the cottage for the line to Shipston. The gentleman on the right was Mr. Vincent, the owner of the cottage. From about 1930, the GWR gradually sold off the land occupied by the tramway. The tramway was officially abandoned by the GWR by an Act of 4th August 1926. This photograph was taken by D. S. Barrie in April 1933.

D. S. Barrie/L & GRP

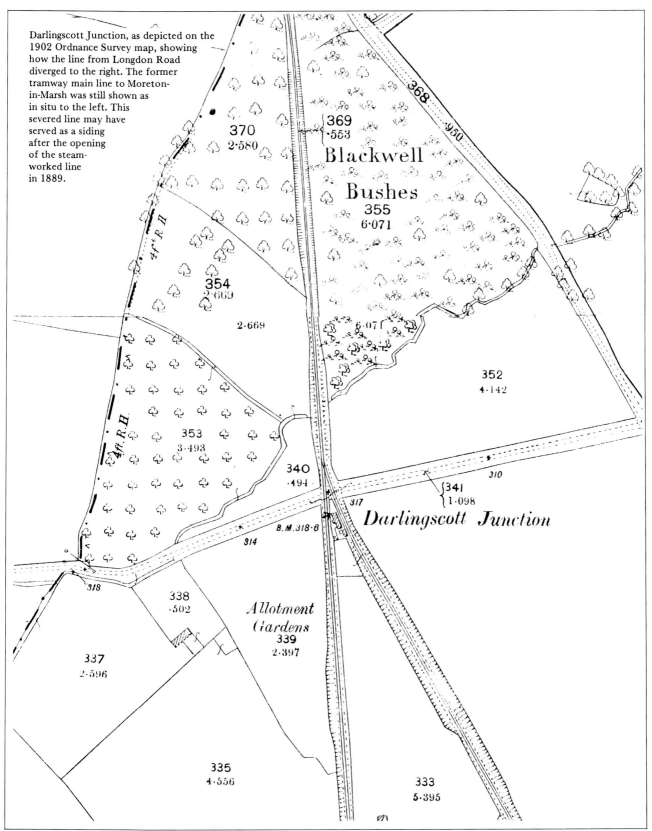

Darlingscott Junction, as depicted on the 1902 Ordnance Survey map, showing how the line from Longdon Road diverged to the right. The former tramway main line to Moreton-in-Marsh was still shown as in situ to the left. This severed line may have served as a siding after the opening of the steam-worked line in 1889.

village of Ilmington could be seen to the left with Ilmington Down (the highest point in Warwickshire) rising to 854ft in the distance. Running beside a country lane, the tramway then turned north-eastwards and, heading across the open fields, eventually reached 'Wharf Inn' and the small complex of tramway buildings at Ilmington Wharf. Here, one of the line's characteristically short passing loops remained *in situ* for many years, though the 1887 Ordnance Survey maps show

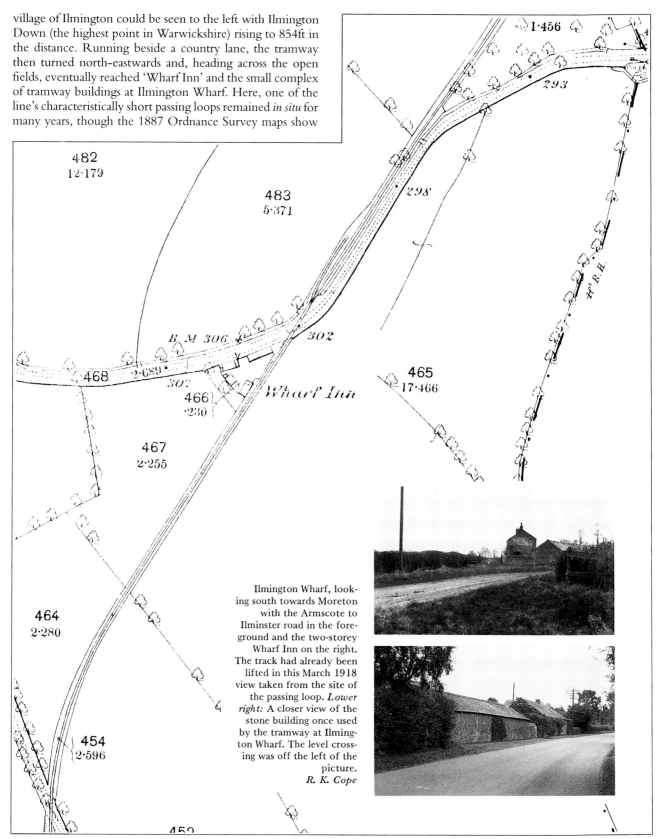

Ilmington Wharf, looking south towards Moreton with the Armscote to Ilminster road in the foreground and the two-storey Wharf Inn on the right. The track had already been lifted in this March 1918 view taken from the site of the passing loop. *Lower right:* A closer view of the stone building once used by the tramway at Ilmington Wharf. The level crossing was off the left of the picture.
R. K. Cope

Taken from 25-inch Ordnance Survey of 1887. Crown copyright reserved.

that it was latterly used as a siding, with no turnout at its northern end.

From Ilmington, the line ran in a north-easterly direction, crossing several fields and eventually reaching the main road at Newbold-on-Stour, where there was another wharf, complete with cottages and warehouses. In its heyday Newbold had been a busy intermediate point on the S & M line, and if small steam engines had ever ventured onto the tramway, Newbold-on-Stour would have been the limit of their northwards progress, for they were legally barred from continuing onto the roadside section beyond.

It is interesting to find that the Railway Clearing House *Handbook of Stations* referred to Newbold Wharf as a 'goods station' during the 1890s, and on this evidence it seems reasonable to conclude that main line goods vehicles were able to reach Newbold-on-Stour at that comparatively late

Newbold Wharf on 3rd March 1918, with the Wharf Cottages on the right and the tramway track still in position. The tramway was not all removed at once, and sections of the tramway evidently survived until 1918. *R. K. Cope*

Looking south from Newbold Wharf on 3rd March 1918. *R. K. Cope*

Taken from 25-inch Ordnance Survey of 1887. Crown copyright reserved.

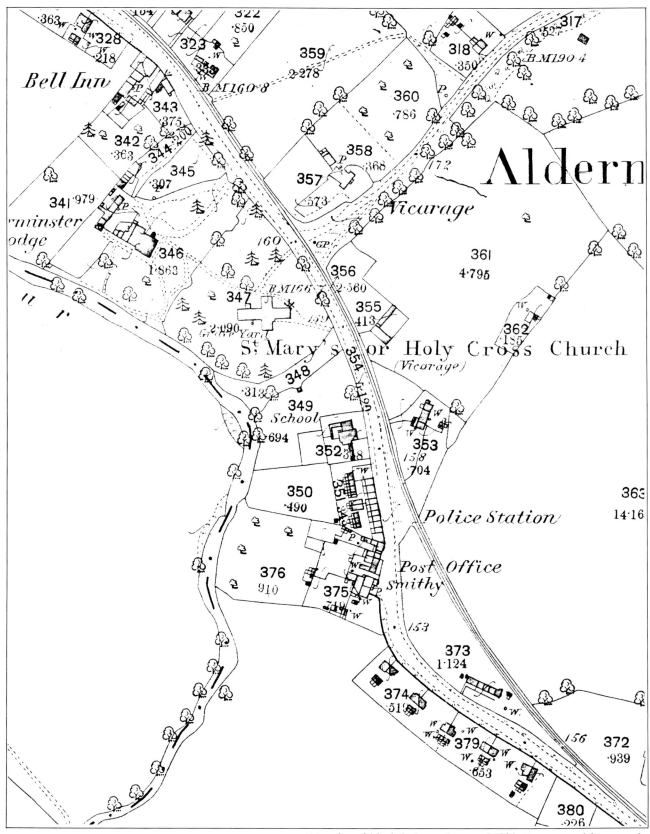

date. The principal source of traffic, in later years at least, was lime from an adjacent lime works.

Curving northwards, the tramway ran beside the Stratford-upon-Avon to Oxford turnpike, and with Ettingham Park visible away to the right, the horse-drawn wagons followed the road for the next two miles or so.

At Alderminster, the line crossed to the right-hand side of the turnpike, and with the red brick houses of this attractive village spread out on either side, the route passed within yards of the parish church. Beyond, the tramway undulated towards Stratford-upon-Avon, crossing to the left-hand side of the road and then passing through some deep cuttings that were spanned, at one point, by an arched bridge carrying a private road to 'Springfield' house.

Nearing Stratford the line crossed the East & West Junction Railway on a road bridge. Although no physical connections were ever established between the two lines, it would have been possible to transfer small consignments between the tramway and nearby Clifford Siding. Sadly,

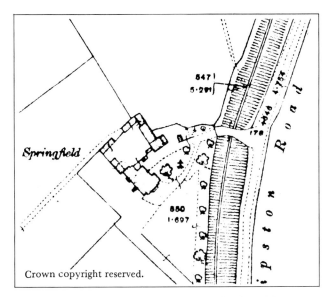

Crown copyright reserved.

For about a mile beyond Clifford Chambers the tramway passed through a cutting which was bridged twice. This c.1902 view shows the red brick arched bridge which carried the driveway diverging from the Shipston Road (now the main Stratford–Oxford road) to a large country residence known as 'Springfield'.   *G. M. Perkins*

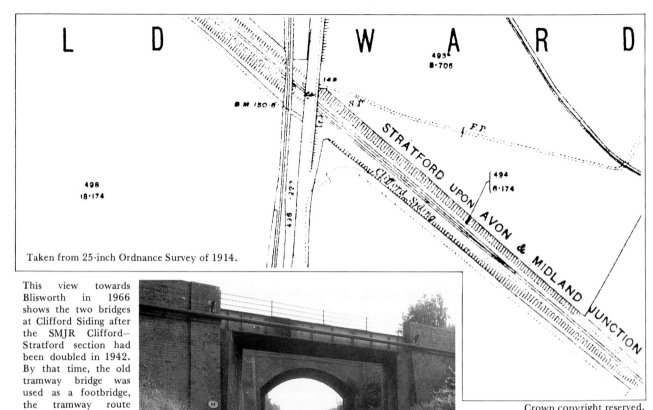

Taken from 25-inch Ordnance Survey of 1914.

This view towards Blisworth in 1966 shows the two bridges at Clifford Siding after the SMJR Clifford–Stratford section had been doubled in 1942. By that time, the old tramway bridge was used as a footbridge, the tramway route from Stratford to a spot just beyond this bridge becoming a public footpath proper c.1934. *R. K. Cope*

The tramway bridge over the East & West Junction line (later SMJR), photographed from the adjacent road overbridge at Clifford Chambers on 30th September 1921. The sleeper-built buffer stop of the SMJ siding can be seen in the right foreground.
R. K. Cope

the East & West Junction never prospered, and its modest passenger services were suspended completely from 1877 until 1885. The Midland and L & NWR companies worked small amounts of goods traffic over the route, but neither company exploited the East & West Junction line to its full potential, and in 1901 an Act was passed enabling the E & WJ to be sold to the Midland, L & NWR, GWR or Manchester Sheffield & Lincolnshire companies. Eventually, on 1st January 1909, the E & WJ was reorganised as an independent company, and having been amalgamated with two other local lines, the company was reborn as 'The Stratford-upon-Avon & Midland Junction Railway'.

The tramway approached Stratford on a long embankment or causeway, which extended for half a mile

The small SMJR goods yard at Clifford Siding, looking east towards Blisworth on 30th September 1921. This picture was taken from the road bridge adjacent to the tramway bridge. When the SMJR line between Stratford and Clifford Siding was later doubled, the goods yard siding was transferred to the top of the shallow cutting on the right. *R. K. Cope*

The Stratford & Moreton Railway embankment, facing Shipston, at the roadside near Stratford on 3rd March 1918. The tramway track had already been removed on this section by this date. *R. K. Cope*

This picture of the tramway occupation underbridge near Middlefield on 3rd March 1918 shows timber decking and brick abutments.
R. K. Cope

across low-lying meadowlands and kept the rails clear of winter flooding. The line parted company with the turnpike as it ran past 'Bridge Town', an outlying part of Stratford, and finally crossed the River Avon on a narrow bridge of nine brick arches. To the right, road traffic crossed the river on an even older stone bridge, dating from the reign of Henry VII. The tramway viaduct was built of English bond brickwork, and had a picturesque toll house at its western end.

Once across the river the line split up into several short branches, giving access to the two canal basins and various lineside industries. One siding ran parallel to Waterside, on the very edge of the town. In common with other early railways, the tramway made considerable use of wagon turntables, enabling sidings to diverge at right-angles to the main lines in order to serve otherwise awkward corners around the basins.

In its early 19th-century heyday the Stratford terminus must have been a place of endless bustle and activity, with wagons being loaded, unloaded, or manhandled around the yard, and narrow boats arriving and departing on the nearby Stratford Canal. The scene would not, however, have been an ugly one – it would have been, as the landscape historian W. G. Hoskins has pointed out, 'a busy landscape, full of detail and movement, like one of Brueghel's paintings'.

There was no connection with either the GWR or S & MJ lines in Stratford, and the tramway was cut off from these other lines by the intervening town. However, main

A view from the southern end of the tramway bridge, looking towards Shipston-on-Stour, during the very hot summer of 1899. This picture provides us with an idea of a typical stretch of the tramway as it would have appeared prior to 1900. The track was deep ballasted to provide a good surface for the horses, and the shine on the rails indicates that this section of the line was still in use.

Benjamin Stone Collection, Birmingham Libraries

The course of the tramway approaching the river bridge, with the sawmill building and chimney in the distance. The photograph was taken on 4th March 1918 shortly before the rails were removed.   *R. K. Cope*

The saw mill, Stratford-upon Avon, viewed from Stratford & Moreton Tramway Bridge on a summer day in 1899. These premises were once served by a tramway siding which terminated adjacent to the curious crane. The cottage on the left was a former toll house. One Stratford-upon-Avon resident clearly recalled playing on the tramway as a child in the 1880s, and hitching rides on 'the tram' to Cox's timber yard. Commodities remembered by him included timber and coal.   *Benjamin Stone Collection, Birmingham Libraries*

line rolling stock would have been worked through from Moreton, if and when such movements were necessary. Later, when the tramway had fallen into a state approaching total dereliction, the infrastructure at Stratford was considerably reduced, and by 1914 only one short siding remained.

It is not possible to give an accurate 'closure date' for the northern section of the tramway, but successive editions of the appropriate 25 inch Ordnance Survey maps hint that the line may simply have fallen into disuse. From time to time, enterprising carriers may have brought one of the old tramway wagons out of retirement in order to carry special loads – and it is possible that sections of the line may have

remained in occasional use, even though through running had ceased. It is, for example, conceivable that coal or other materials could have been off-loaded from canal boats at Stratford and taken down to Clifford Siding or Alderminster on 'the tram'.

The tramway was certainly in operation as a through route in the 1880s, and it is known that loads of coal were taken south to Moreton-in-Marsh until about 1885. In the reverse direction, timber seems to have been carried back to Stratford, and it may be no coincidence that the last remaining siding at that place gave access to the premises of a timber merchant.

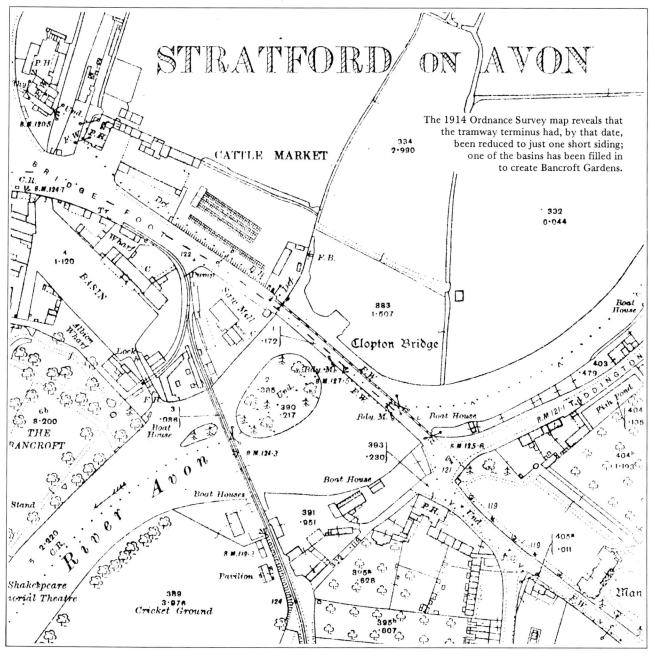

The 1914 Ordnance Survey map reveals that the tramway terminus had, by that date, been reduced to just one short siding; one of the basins has been filled in to create Bancroft Gardens.

A panoramic view of the station from the buffer stops c.1950. The somewhat forlorn appearance of the station site was improved by the clean and tidy permanent way. The two 'Iron Mink' vans on the left were used for storage.

M. E. J. Deane

CHAPTER SIX

THE BRITISH RAILWAYS ERA
(1948-1963)

An unidentified '2301' class 0–6–0 shunting at Shipston c.1949. According to the summer 1947 working timetable, 'only engines of the 2301, 0–6–0 class (uncoloured) are authorised to work over this branch'. The duty covering the branch at that time was similar to 1936, a Worcester engine and crew working as follows: 4.55 a.m. Worcester–Moreton Goods, shunt at Moreton, 9.30 a.m. goods to Campden and back, shunt at Moreton, 1.0 p.m. Moreton–Shipston, 3.30 p.m. Shipston–Moreton, 5.45 p.m. Moreton–Campden Eng & Van, 6.20 p.m. Campden–Kingham Pilot Trip, 6.55 p.m. Kingham–Moreton Pilot Trip, 8.40 p.m. Lt. Eng. Moreton–Worcester. *J. H. Russell*

THE end of the war in Europe was followed by the election of a Labour government in July 1945, and this new administration lost no time in putting an ambitious nationalisation programme into effect. It was considered that by bringing the 'commanding heights of the economy' into public ownership, the misery of mass unemployment would become a thing of the past, and on 1st January 1948 a nationwide fanfare of locomotive whistles heralded the demise of the Big Four railway companies created in 1923. Henceforth, the railway system would be administered by a new, nationwide organisation known as British Railways.

In reality, the advent of public ownership made little difference to rural outposts such as the Shipston-on-Stour branch, and life at Shipston went on much as before. The station master at that time was Cyril Smith, who had worked at the station since 1943 and was destined to remain until closure. Other locally-employed staff included female lorry driver Mrs Turville, whose railway career had commenced in World War Two, and Harry Bradley in the goods department. The son of a railway delivery driver, Mr Bradley was himself employed as a driver during the war, but he subsequently worked as a checker.

The Shipston branch guard, from the 1930s onwards, was Fred Perry of Moreton-in-Marsh, while Bernard E. Hardiman, also of Moreton, was a regular locomotive driver. Other guards, around 1950, included Frank Curtis of Moreton and Ernest Talbot of Kingham, while Fred Gubbins

and Ken Hughes were both regular footplatemen during the final years of operation.

POST-WAR TRAFFIC

The line enjoyed a modest revival in the years immediately following World War Two. With petrol rationing still strictly enforced, and a Labour government which remained fully committed to the concept of a fully-integrated transport system, Shipston goods yard was invariably full of wagons or vans waiting to be loaded or unloaded. Coal still provided a major source of bulk traffic, but there were, in addition, certain new types of traffic such as fertilizers for use on local farms, and wagon loads of 40ft reinforcing bars for Beecham Buildings Ltd, a reinforced concrete firm. In 1959, a Suffolk farmer moved his entire stock of agricultural machinery from Lavenham to Shipston-on-Stour, and it was necessary to run a special freight train consisting of fourteen machinery-carrying wagons, which arrived at the terminus on 11th May .

The branch remained relatively busy throughout the late 1950s, and although road transport had started to threaten the line's primary sources of traffic, the Shipston-on-Stour 'Wagons Forwarded & Received Book' reveals that up to fifty wagon loads of coal or coke were still arriving in the station every month. In March 1959, for example, the station handled 54 wagons of coal together with no less than 30 wagons of fertilizer, while in the following June Shipston dealt with 51 wagons of coal, 5 wagons of fertilizer, 6 wagons

95

Dean Goods 0—6—0 No. 2458 at Shipston-on-Stour on 2nd July 1953 in readiness for the return journey to Moreton with the branch freight.

N. E. Preedy

of machinery, 1 wagon load of cattle feed, 1 bogie steel vehicle, and 13 wagon loads of miscellaneous goods.

The 'Wagons Forwarded & Received Book' provided a valuable record of the types of traffic handled at Shipston during its declining years, and it would be useful to show at least some of this interesting data in tabular form. The following table has been compiled from material held by the Shipston Local History Society.

POST-WAR MOTIVE POWER

Because of their light axle loading, 0-6-0 Dean Goods loco-motives continued to work the branch during the early years of nationalisation, particularly Nos. 2339, 2458 and 2551. B. J. Penney (then an apprentice at Worcester) recalled that when, in December 1951, the Worcester breakdown train was sent to rerail a brake van in Shipston yard, the train engine, a 57xx pannier, was not allowed to enter the branch because of its axle loading, so No 2551 was specially sent from Kingham to work the train for the remainder of the journey to Shipston-on-Stour.

Writing in the Autumn 1986 *British Railways Journal*, Mr Penney also recalled that, for operating purposes, the branch officially 'began' on the far side of Todenham Road crossing, the section on the station side being classified as part of

TABLE 6: WAGONS RECEIVED AT SHIPSTON-ON-STOUR BETWEEN NOV. 1958 & MAY 1960						
Date	Coal & Coke	Fertilizer or cattle feed	Mach-inery	Steel bars	Miscell-aneous	Totals
Nov 58	50	18	4	-	11	83
Dec 58	44	14	1	1	18	78
Jan 59	38	8	-	2	3	51
Feb 59	47	22	-	2	9	80
Mar 59	54	30	4	-	12	100
Apr 59	34	12	7	1	6	60
May 59	50	5	19	-	11	85
Jun 59	51	6	6	1	13	77
Jul 59	41	3	-	-	6	50
Aug 59	26	6	1	-	6	39
Sep 59	49	13	2	-	13	77
Oct 59	44	27	-	1	9	81
Nov 59	25	7	4	1	8	45
Dec 59	22	29	-	5	4	60
Jan 60	31	15	-	2	3	51
Feb 60	30	16	3	3	3	55
Mar 60	55	33	4	3	3	110
Apr 60	16	8	2	3	3	32
May 60	3	1	-	-	-	4

NB The figures for April & May 1960 are unusually low because of the impending closure of the branch. Conversely, the noticeably high totals for March 1959 and March 1960 reflect large consignments of coal brought in readiness for the following winter.

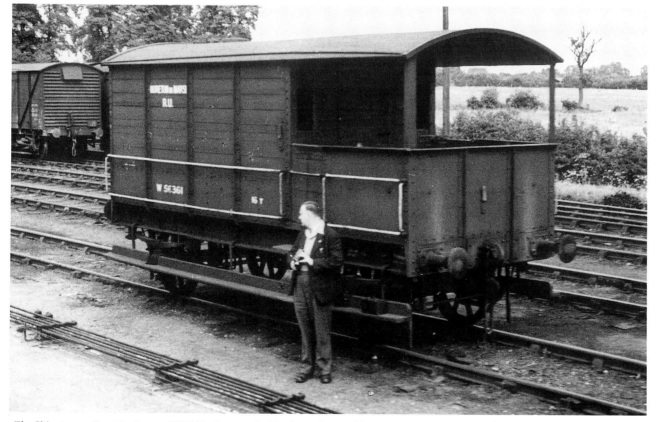

The Shipston-on-Stour brake van W56361 photographed in the exchange sidings at Moreton-in-Marsh on 31st August 1952.

H. F. Wheeller

Moreton yard. When a Shipston-bound train entered the branch, the level crossing gates at Todenham Road were locked behind it and the key was returned to Moreton-in-Marsh signal box, and having been 'locked-in' to the Shipston line, the train resumed its journey, all other crossing gates being unlocked by a key on the single line staff. Generally speaking, the gates were unlocked by the fireman and closed by the guard, who was provided with a separate key in order that the gates could be locked behind the train.

Hinting that in its last years the branch was worked in a somewhat unorthodox manner, Mr Penney has suggested that some train crews were not averse to stopping for a quick pint at the Golden Cross Inn at Stretton-on-Fosse, an exceed-ingly rural establishment in which free bread and cheese was often supplied to customers purchasing a pint! Another entertaining story concerns a train which ran through one of the intermediate crossing gates, and it would perhaps be best to let Mr Penney tell this tale in his own words:

'The story I best recall concerns a Worcester driver, not very familiar with working the branch, who was charged with running through the gates at an intermediate crossing. His written reply states that when proceeding along the branch, tender first on the Dean Goods, the train ran into a swarm of bees which immediately took possession of the cab, forcing himself and his fireman to quickly vacate it along the side framing, to take refuge in front of the smokebox. The train, meanwhile, proceeded on its way and although the swarm eventually flew off, he and his mate were unable to get back into the cab quickly enough to prevent the train running through the crossing gates. There

Ex-MSWJR 2–4–0 No. 1335 at Stretton-on-Fosse station on the way to Shipston with the Stephenson Locomotive Society Shipston Special on 31st August 1952.   *P. J. Garland*

Stretton-on-Fosse station in its declining years, taken from the brake van of a Shipston–Moreton goods on 2nd July 1953. By this time, the station building and siding had been removed, although the weighbridge office and part of the loading gauge remained. The land behind the platform was in use as allotments.   *Collection R. S. Carpenter*

were no independent witnesses to corroborate this statement and there is no record to say whether this explanation was accepted by the District Superintendent!'

The three Dean Goods 0-6-0s lasted until 1953-4, the first to go being Nos. 2339 and 2551 in the summer of 1953; No 2458 remained at Worcester until the following January, by which time three standard class 2MT 2-6-0s had arrived in the area. The new arrivals were Nos. 78004, 78008 and 78009, all of which saw service on the Shipston branch. One of the engines was usually sub-shedded at Kingham from where it worked both the Shipston-on-Stour and Chipping Norton branches. Another type of engine seen on the line during the BR era were the 16xx panniers which, with their 4ft 1½in wheels and light axle loadings, were the lineal descendants of the lightweight saddle tanks used prior to World War One.

One or two enthusiasts' specials traversed the branch during the 1950s, and these sporadic excursions brought passenger trains back to Shipston some twenty years after the premature cessation of regular services. On 31st August 1952,

for instance, ex-Midland & South Western Junction 2-4-0 No 1335 worked a four-coach Stephenson Locomotive Society special over the line, while Dean Goods 0-6-0 No 2474 hauled a similar train on 24th April 1955. An earlier special, which had visited the branch on 24th May 1952, was notable in that it had brought a streamlined GWR diesel railcar to Shipston for the first, and indeed the last, time. This particular trip was organised by the Birmingham Locomotive Club, and the car involved was GWR railcar No 14. A further special traversed the branch in July 1958, when a party of twenty-one enthusiasts rode over the line in a brake van special. The locomotive on that occasion was one of the usual branch 2-6-0s, and its driver was Bernard Hardiman of Moreton-in-Marsh.

THE FINAL YEARS
The appearance of such special workings brought a modicum of interest and variety to the tranquil Shipston-on-Stour branch line, but there could be no doubt that by the late 1950s BR was preparing to close this historic route. The days

BR Standard class 2 2–6–0 No. 78009 approaching Stretton-on-Fosse station with a Shipston-bound freight on 6th October 1953.

G. Bannister

when small consignments of wagon-load traffic could sustain a rural branch were gone for ever, and faced by increasing competition from road transport, BR realised that its railway network would survive only if it concentrated on certain special types of business, notably Inter-City passenger travel and train-load freight traffic. The archaic Shipston branch clearly did not fit into this new pattern, and, with small wagon-load goods depots closing all over the country, BR announced that the railway between Moreton-in-Marsh and Shipston would be closed 'on and from 2nd May 1960'.

Alternative facilities for coal and wagon-load traffic were available at Stratford where, suggested the closure notices, Shipston traders could still make use of Old Town depot and Clifford Siding. There was, significantly, no mention of the still-extant freight depot at Moreton-in-Marsh (Stratford, rather than Moreton being the 'natural' shopping and trading centre for Shipston residents).

Station master Cyril Smith was offered a temporary appointment at Stratford-upon-Avon, but goods checker Harry Bradley was able to continue in his job at Shipston, where arrangements for the collection and delivery of parcels and 'smalls' traffic were scheduled to continue, at least for a few more months.

The station was closed officially on Monday, 2nd May, the last incoming freight train having arrived at Shipston at 10.30am on the preceding Thursday (ie 28th April). This final down working was driven by Bernard Hardiman and fired by Ken Hughes. The guard was another regular in the person of Fred Curtis. Appropriately, the return trip to Moreton was made in the fast time of 42 minutes, and the class 4MT 2-6-0 and its short train arrived back at the junction by 11.37am.

The 'last' train was accompanied by local reporter V. J. Davis, who noted that the 2-6-0 'scuttled willingly round the bends as if pleased at changing its usual crawl to a dash'. Rounding Longdon curve, he was able to glimpse 'the old horse tramway and, in the distance . . . Junction Cottage marooned in a field, forgotten'. Passing Stretton-on-Fosse, the train was soon clattering over the Knee Brook, and all too soon, the engine was whistling for the gates to be opened at Todenham Road.

Although Shipston-on-Stour station was 'closed' on Monday, 2nd May, the last train actually ran on Tuesday the 3rd when a locomotive passed over the branch for the very last time in order to clear the empty wagons for Shipston yard. Having performed this melancholy task, it returned to Moreton-in-Marsh, thereby bringing 134 years of railway history to a close.

The parcels office at Shipston remained open for a few months thereafter, but finally, in May 1963, these residual facilities were withdrawn, and Shipston's links with the railway age were ended for ever. In the meantime, track lifting operations had commenced in the summer of 1961, and the line was soon cut back to Stretton-on-Fosse. The work of destruction continued into the early months of 1962, until, by the following summer, the branch had been reduced to a truncated spur beside the empty branch platform at Moreton-in-Marsh.

The alternative facilities at Stratford lasted only a few months longer, and on 1st March 1965 the Stratford-upon-Avon to Burton Dassett section of the former East & West Junction Railway was closed 'temporarily', followed by an official closure on 5th July. Moreton-in-Marsh, meanwhile, remained open for both passenger and freight traffic,

The remains of Longdon Road station during its declining years, viewed from the brake van of the Shipston–Moreton goods, 2nd July 1953.
R. S. Carpenter

becoming a useful railhead for the surrounding area and handling over 60,000 passengers a year. In 1979, for example, the station dealt with 68,193 passengers – over three times as many as in 1930. Freight traffic, however, was less healthy, and after a period of decline the station's coal yard and goods depot were closed, leaving Moreton as a passenger-only station.

THE RAILWAY TODAY

Disused railways can usually be followed on foot or by road, and this is certainly the case with the Shipston-on-Stour branch and its northwards continuation to Stratford. Indeed, the abandoned trackbed of these two lines still retains much of interest for the dedicated walker or industrial archaeologist.

At Moreton-in-Marsh, the former tramway terminus could still be seen in the 1980s, and although the nearby 'One' and 'Two' coal sidings had been removed, the position of the surviving tramway buildings provided a visual indication of how the 1826 terminus was arranged (i.e. at an angle to the present main line).

Unfortunately, the yard in which the terminal buildings were situated was sold by BR, and the new owners of the site decided to demolish the tramway buildings to make room for a vast concrete supermarket; the historic tramway terminus was therefore destroyed in its entirety, this melancholy task being accomplished on 7th and 8th April 1989.

Despite this loss, it is of interest that, even at the time of writing, the remaining stub of the Shipston branch still leaves Moreton up platform, and the downside station buildings and the standard GWR signal box have survived more or less unchanged.

From Moreton the line continues, past Todenham Lane crossing cottage, and the adjacent A429 provides a convenient route towards Stretton-on-Fosse. Here the Golden Cross Inn is in use as a private house, although the station itself has disappeared. A similar situation pertains at Longdon Road, where the timber station buildings have been removed, leaving, however, the brick arches which formerly supported the vanished booking office and waiting room. The neighbouring station master's cottage remains in being as a dwelling house, and the overall arrangement of the abandoned station is still fairly clear.

One of the interesting aspects of the Shipston line is the way in which the late-Victorian 'steam tramway' utilised as much as possible of the earlier horse line, and for this reason it is possible, even today, for diligent searchers to locate substantial fragments of John Rastrick's original engineering works. Many of the surviving bridges, for instance, incorporate sections of stone walling that are clearly relics of the old tramway, while at Longdon Road the embankment needed to lift the railway above surrounding meadowlands is supported, for much of its length, on a sort of dry-stone wall that recalls the famous 'cob' at Portmadoc. Such construction methods would not have been used in the 1880s, but the old walling was perfectly adequate as a means of support for the later railway, and the Great Western engineers who rebuilt the line were obviously content to let it remain *in situ* beneath their new station.

The line continues unimpeded towards Shipston where, sadly, most of the terminus has been demolished, but there is consolation on the remaining sections of the Stratford line, which have retained many recognisable features, including 'Junction Cottage' and the wharf buildings at Ilmington and Newbold.

Moving northwards to Stratford-upon-Avon, we find further relics of the tramway, including the impressive arched bridge across the River Avon, a long embankment on the approach to the river, and last but not least, a perfectly preserved tramway wagon standing on its own section of 1820s-type permanent way. Nearby, the site of an extensive canal basin is now occupied by an attractive open space known as Bancroft Gardens, but several identifiable buildings can be discerned, and it is possible (with the aid of the maps reproduced in this book) for readers to obtain a good idea of what the northern terminus of the Stratford & Moreton Railway must have looked like in its early 19th century prime.

THE S & MR WAGON

The vehicle now preserved at Stratford is not the only S & MR wagon in existence, but it is the only one accessible to the general public, and it would therefore be fitting to conclude with a few notes on this historic vehicle.

The wagon is of standard gauge, and conforms, in its essentials, to a prototype 'Testing Carriage' designed by John Rastrick during the early stages of construction (see illustration on page 18 of *The Stratford & Moreton Tramway* by John Norris).

The wagon consists of a stoutly-constructed chassis formed of two longitudinal solebars which are maintained in position by cross members and the 3½ inch diameter axles beneath. The wheels are of 3ft diameter, and the body is formed of four horizontal planks. The resulting vehicle looks something like a farm wagon, and this resemblance is accentuated by 7in 'outraves' attached to the top planks. The overall length of the wagon is little over 11ft, while its maximum width (over the wheel bosses) is about 4ft 10ins. There are hinged tail boards at each end, and the height above ground level is 1ft 10ins – horses would thus have been able to jump aboard with very little effort. Now restored in a natural wood finish, the wagon was once lettered 'THOMAS HUTCHINGS, NEWBOLD LIMEWORKS', and this inscription provides a clue as to the traffic carried on the line towards the end of its life.

The wagon was saved from scrap in 1935 as a result of efforts made by the Trustees & Guardians of the Shakespeare Birthplace Trust, who persuaded the local authorities to have the vehicle preserved and mounted on the site of the Stratford & Moreton Railway terminus at Stratford.

Stratford & Moreton Tramway wagon photographed on 15th May 1942.
V. R. Webster

Appendix 1
SOME PROMINENT PERSONALITIES

William James (1771-1837): Born on 13th June 1871, William James trained as a solicitor and subsequently worked as a land agent for the Earl of Warwick. A prominent colliery owner and canal promoter, he was, at one time, chairman of the West Bromwich Coalmasters' Association. On becoming interested in railways he obtained a 25 per cent interest in Stephenson's locomotive patents, and undertook to give his 'best assistance for the using and employing of locomotive engines south of an imaginary line drawn from Liverpool to Hull'. William James is best described as a visionary rather than a practical engineer, but he nevertheless surveyed several early lines including the Liverpool & Manchester Railway. His association with the Stephensons was not entirely happy, and he later claimed that Robert Stephenson had used many of his ideas. Today, James is best remembered for his achievements in connection with the Stratford & Moreton Railway. He died, in unhappy circumstances, in March 1837.

John Urpeth Rastrick (1780-1856): Although J. U. Rastrick was an important figure during the early days of railway construction, he has not enjoyed the kind of recognition afforded to certain of his contemporaries. Like Brunel, John Rastrick was interested in mechanical *and* civil engineering, and in 1817 he was made managing partner in the engineering firm of Bradley, Foster & Rastrick, a Stourbridge firm whose pioneer locomotive *Stourbridge Lion* was the first railway engine to run in the United States of America. Rastrick was prominently associated with the Stratford & Moreton Railway, and he probably designed most, if not all, of its engineering features. He was also associated with the interesting though little-known Shutt End Railway, but is best remembered for his work as engineer of the London to Brighton line.

Thomas Telford (1757-1834): A Scotsman, Thomas Telford is rightly regarded as one of the great civil engineers, and his many works include the Holyhead Road, the Menai and Conway road bridges and the Caledonian Canal. He is best known as a road and canal engineer, but acted as consultant during the construction of the Stratford & Moreton Railway.

Isambard Kingdom Brunel (1801-1859): Often regarded as the greatest civil and marine engineer of the Victorian era, I. K. Brunel was one of the most remarkable men of his day. As engineer to the Great Western Railway, he automatically became engineer to the Oxford Worcester & Wolverhampton Railway when that company was formed in the 1840s, and in this capacity Brunel suggested that the Stratford & Moreton might be adapted for use as a steam railway. As OW & WR engineer he also designed the still-extant station at Moreton-in-Marsh – although it should be stressed that little of his work can now be seen at Moreton apart from the actual line and a stone-built overbridge.

John Fowler (1817-1898): Engineer to the OW & WR and later consulting engineer to the GWR, John Fowler was associated with several important projects including the Metropolitan Railway, the Severn Tunnel and the Forth Bridge.

John Freeman Mitford (1748-1830): A former Lord Chancellor of Ireland, John Freeman Mitford, the first Baron Redesdale, was a major supporter of the Stratford & Moreton Railway, which he clearly saw as a means of helping his tenants and improving his estate at Batsford, near Moreton-in-Marsh.

John Thomas Freeman Mitford (1805-1886): The second Lord Redesdale took a great interest in the work of the House of Lords, and did much to enhance the reputation of the Upper House. A stickler for detail, Robert Hudson remembered him as 'the terror of all who had to pass the ordeal of standing orders'. Railway Bills were one of his specialities, and although his attitude to the Oxford Worcester & Wolverhampton Railway was sometimes ambiguous, he inevitably became a major supporter both of that undertaking and of its parent company, the GWR. Hudson suggested that he 'continued to take a paternal interest in the Stratford & Moreton Railway' and this interest may explain why the Great Western was reluctant to abandon the tramway even though its useful life had long since passed. It might be added that the famous Mitford sisters - one of whom was a close friend of Adolf Hitler – were relatives of the 19th century Redesdales.

Robert Hudson: A Great Western official who was responsible for both the Stratford & Moreton Railway and the railway-owned Stratford Canal, Robert Hudson seems to have taken a keen interest in the tramway, and one senses, from his writings on the subject, that he must have been a sort of Victorian railway enthusiast. H. Weaver, who supervised the tramway from about 1881, recalled that Mr Hudson 'was much respected throughout the district for his business ability, and he also had quite a literary reputation'. Hudson's first-hand account of a journey over the tramway in the late 1850s (quoted in Chapter 2) is a valuable record of the Stratford & Moreton Railway written by one who knew it well.

FURTHER READING

The literature of the Stratford & Moreton Railway has not been extensive, and some of the works listed below may not be easily available. It was felt, however, that some form of bibliography might be of use to local historians seeking a guide to further study, and it is hoped that the following list will be of at least some interest to other scholars.

Robert Hudson, 'The Story of the Stratford-on-Avon & Moreton Railway', *Great Western Railway Magazine*, March 1889

Vivian Bird, 'Even the Horse Rode Downhill', *The Sunday Mercury*, 30th August 1964

Charles Lines, 'For Enthusiasts Only', *The Coventry Evening Telegraph*, 1st December 1961

Stanley C. Jenkins, 'The Shipston-on-Stour Branch, *British Railways Journal*, Summer 1986, No.12

S. C. Jenkins and H. I. Quayle, 'The Oxford, Worcester & Wolverhampton Railway' Oakwood Press (1977)

Ken Werrett, 'Stratford & Moreton Tramway Mineral Wagon', *Model Railway News*, November 1964

D. S. Barrie, 'The Stratford & Moreton Railway', *The Railway Magazine*, February 1935

Charles Hadfield & John Norris, *Waterways to Stratford* , David & Charles (1962)

F. T. S. Houghton, *The Little Guide to Worcestershire* , Methuen (1922)

John Norris, *The Stratford & Moreton Tramway* (Railway & Canal Historical Society, 1987)

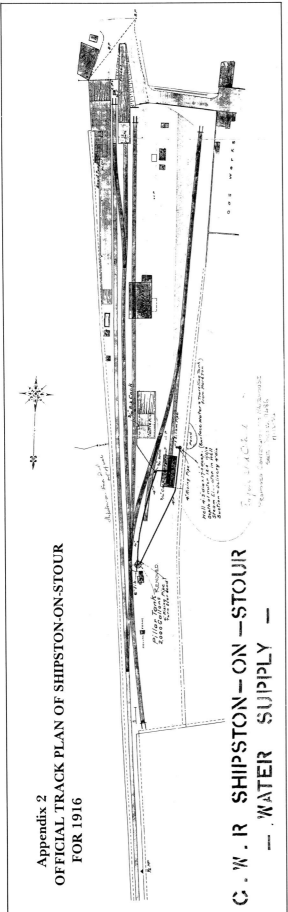

Appendix 2

OFFICIAL TRACK PLAN OF SHIPSTON-ON-STOUR FOR 1916

G. W. R SHIPSTON—ON—STOUR

— WATER SUPPLY —

Appendix 3

MINISTRY OF TRANSPORT REPORT ON THE VELOCIPEDE ACCIDENT NEAR LONGDON ROAD

SIR,

I have the honour to report for the information of the Minister of Transport, in accordance with the Order of the 5th March, the result of my Inquiry into the circumstances attending the fatal accident which occurred on the 3rd February, 1930, to C. Webb near Longdon Road on the Great Western Railway.

Webb was employed as a ganger on the Stretton-on-Fosse to Shipston-on-Stour section of the single line steam tramway from Moreton-in-Marsh to Shipston-on-Stour. The branch is some eight miles in length and is worked with one engine in steam or two engines coupled together. Instructions are laid down in the Sectional Appendix that each ganger must inspect his own length daily, using a velocipede inspection car. When using the car the ganger must obtain permission from the stationmaster in the direction from which the next train is due to arrive. Telephones are provided in huts at eight points on the branch for the purpose, as also at the four stations. Further, it is distinctly stipulated that on no account must either of the gangers, of whom there are two on the branch, take his car or trolley beyond Stretton-on-Fosse, the intermediate station on the branch. Only one regular booked train daily is worked over the branch, which is timed to leave Moreton-in-Marsh at 1.35 p.m. To avoid the necessity of sending out the necessary flagmen when the car or a trolley is placed on the line, in accordance with Rule 247, etc., the Engineering Department are given absolute occupation of the line between Moreton-in-Marsh and Shipston-on-Stour after the arrival of the last train at the former station and until 15 minutes before the first train is due to leave Moreton-in-Marsh the following morning. No special train must be run without notice having been given to the gangers and acknowledged by them.

It would appear that Webb, who was ganger on the upper section, placed the velocipede inspection car on the line about 1.40 p.m. at the permanent way hut, a little over a mile on the Shipston side of Stretton-on-Fosse Station. He was last seen by his sub-ganger, Edward Hands, at that point when Hands and the other two members of the gang left to commence hedge cutting duties. The daily goods train, consisting of nine wagons and brake van, due to leave Moreton-in-Marsh at 1.35 p.m., was despatched at 1.25 p.m. It arrived at Stretton-on-Fosse, the intermediate station, at 1.45 p.m. and left at 1.55 p.m., being then 15 minutes before time. On approaching Longdon Road the driver, F. W. Gubbins, sighted the velocipede in front proceeding in the same direction. It was then about 20 yards in advance, Webb being upon it with his back towards the following train. The whistle is stated to have been sounded and every effort made both to attract Webb's attention and stop the train, but without avail, and the velocipede was struck by the engine. Webb was thrown from it and run over with fatal results. Gubbins states that on application of the brake all the engine wheels picked up, thus preventing him from stopping earlier.

The unfortunate occurrence arose through a failure on the part of Webb to observe the instructions laid down, but which I feel have been somewhat neglected in the past. He neither made use of the telephone to obtain permission to occupy the line nor, failing that, did he arrange to provide a flagman. His sub-ganger was not aware of these instructions until after the occurrence. The despatch of the train before time, though by no means an uncommon procedure, possibly led to a feeling of false security in Webb's mind. The train was running at a low speed, stated to have been 5 m.p.h. Unfortunately, owing to the fact that the engine was running bunker first, the velocipede was not sighted by the driver until he was within some 20 yards of it. The line approaching the point where the accident took place is laid on curves of 10, 11 and 24 chains to the right. Gubbins was on the left side of his engine in the direction of travel, and the bunker would obscure his view, but on the other side had his fireman been disengaged, and looking out, the velocipede could have been sighted from a point quite 120 yards away and in ample time to avoid coming in contact with it.

No doubt as a result of the regrettable occurrence greater care will be exercised by all concerned to regard strictly the regulations relating to the working of the branch in future. Steps should be taken to ensure that all the staff engaged thereon are thoroughly acquainted with them, and impressed with the fact that no trolley or velocipede must be placed upon the line, unless the usual flagmen are provided, until sanction has been obtained from a responsible authority. Also, as the timing of the departure of the train from Moreton-in-Marsh is of vital importance, measures should be taken to see that such timing is rigidly enforced.

Webb had been on duty seven hours when the occurrence took place.

I have, etc.,

J. P. S. MAIN.

Appendix 4
THE STRATFORD TERMINUS OF THE STRATFORD & MORETON TRAMWAY
as shown on the 1852 Ordnance Survey

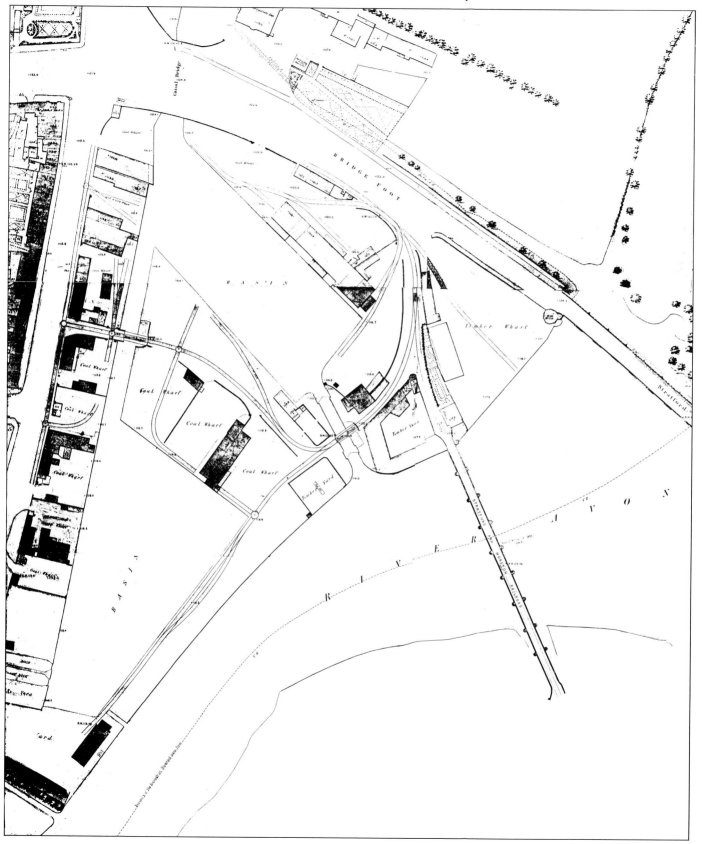

Appendix 5
THE STRATFORD TERMINUS OF THE STRATFORD & MORETON TRAMWAY
as shown on the 1886 25-inch Ordnance Survey

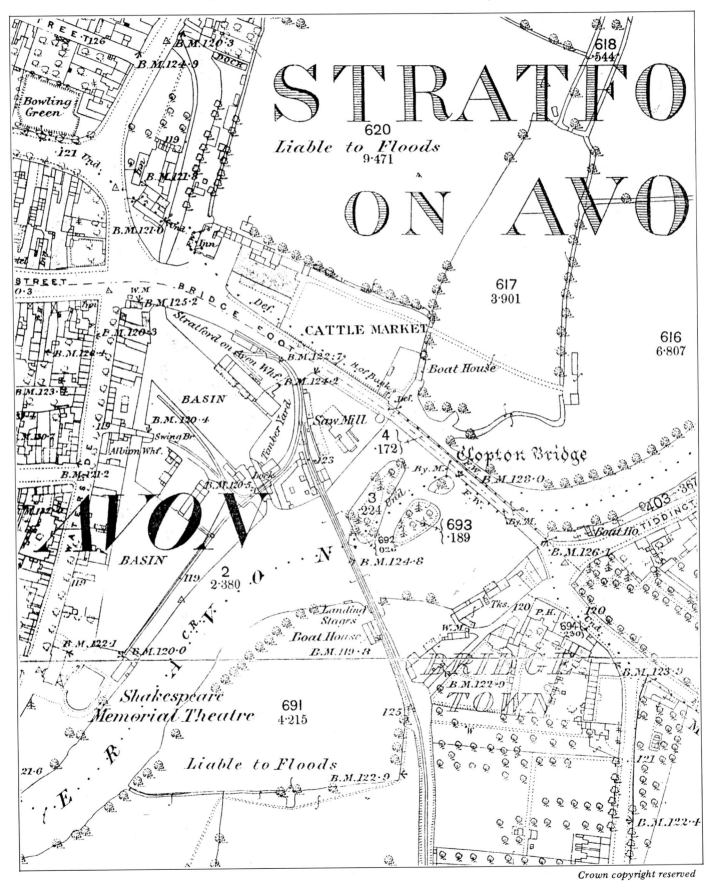